M000223651

WHAT OTHERS ARE SAYING ABOUT CHRISTINE MILES AND THIS BOOK

"Christine was essential to pulling off a virtual summit, launched just as COVID hit, that attracted thousands of people across all continents and raised $180,000 for charity. Her intuitive gift of listening to the story behind the story as she coached some of today's most influential management thinkers resulted in presentations that led even these highly experienced public speakers to new realms of authenticity and personal connection. She has a gift."

— Kaihan Krippendorff
Founder, Outthinker

"Christine has transformed the way we listen. No longer do we focus on the solution but more on the beginning and struggles of our customers. This way we fully understand what our customer is looking to achieve and can tailor a solution to meet their desired outcome. Christine Miles' Listening Path is a game changer in life and business. Christine makes it simple to listen with six questions and the Listening Path."

— Justin Barr
Partner/Founder, Clear Process Solutions

"I have worked with Christine for sixteen years as a coach, consultant, and trainer. When I met Christine, we started our journey as a one-on-one executive coaching partnership that led me down a path of understanding my why, asking a lot more questions, story development, and truly listening to what others have to say. Our success together led to our organization expanding Christine's influence to include our leadership team and other key bench members throughout our organization. Christine has taken us through many team-building experiences that helped create a true emotional connection between the individuals and our teams, which led to better teaming and increased business. Christine has helped us see our way through the tearing down of departmental walls, which enriched our culture of caring about each other, the community, and our environment. I can't thank Christine enough for how she has helped me be a better leader, boss, friend, teammate, dad, husband, and person."

— Frank Rhea
Executive Vice President, Tozour Energy Systems

"Nobody, nobody *understands* as well as Christine. Coupled with Christine's ability to understand the human condition is her intuitive understanding of business. How do I know? Together, we created the number-one business radio show in the country and have interviewed 10,000+ CEOs. These CEOs have repeatedly told me that Christine is 'incredible,' and they often have engaged Christine's counsel—and most important, continue to engage Christine's counsel. She is a force of nature. If you're fortunate, you'll get a dose of Christine."

— Herb Cohen
CEO, Executive Leaders Radio

"I have worked with Christine for ten years as my leadership coach. She taught me that school leadership and management is, at heart, about 'gathering' through listening and understanding people's stories. In doing so, it becomes possible to build the story of the organization, the vision, and the strategy that are necessary for facilitating growth, change, and the greatness of others."

— Sue Szczepkowski
Head of Lower School, Germantown Academy

"Hearing is not listening and the results of the two could not be more different. Christine demonstrates this in her actions and teaches this in a way that is both relatable and practical. Transformational Listening is not just a valuable skill to learn—it is a necessary one."

— Kyle Bray
Chief Operating Officer, Consumer Medical

"Christine has positively changed my behavior and ability to listen more than I talk. My wife has noticed a significant change in my patience; I focus on what she is saying, and only reply after she is done talking with positive comments and an acknowledgment that I did, in fact, not only hear her but listened. I highly recommend taking the time to read her book and have her as a guest speaker because she gets everyone involved."

— Kevin Nally
CIO, US Secret Service

"Many of us know that seeking first to understand is often the first step in generating positive outcomes. What Christine has developed with her Story Gathering approach is how to do that well—a way that is effective in creating beneficial understanding for both the one asking the questions, as well as the one answering them."

— Dan Brewer
Chief Resource Officer, Brewer Science

"We are so fortunate to have had Christine Miles speak to our business students several times, sharing her amazing life lessons, many of which demonstrate the art and power of being a tuned-in listener. Her new book is a must read for people from all walks of life, and one I intend to get into the hands of as many of our students as possible."

— Sue Lehrman
Dean, Rohrer College of Business, Rowan University

"Christine nails the missing and most important piece in communications—listening. I've witnessed how deeply she listens and to how she listens to the way she listens when she interacts with you. Translating this into a book for anyone interested is a gift to your life I wholeheartedly champion."

— Dr. Perpetua Neo
Executive Coach and Psychologist

"I first met Christine Miles several years ago when she was the featured speaker at an IT Conference in Atlanta. She had two spots on the agenda, and I had volunteered to be one of the panelists she interviewed in her first session. I still have my notes from her presentation and refer to them frequently to ensure I am asking the right questions and listening to understand what is being said; not just hearing an answer. 'Tell me more' and 'Then what happened?' have enabled me to get all the facts. I can honestly say she has had a huge impact on my success."

— Lee W. Crump
Managing Partner, The Crump Group, LLC

"It may be more important than ever to make a conscious decision to seek to understand others. To do that we need to know how to listen. Christine's approach is both brilliant and simple."

— Ann Hook
COO, SolomonEdwards

"Christine Miles has provided excellent perspective for me during the last three years as an executive coach who models the very listening skills with me that she works so hard to help others to develop through her Listening Path model. This model is both accessible for people of varying age ranges and aligns well with the work of diversity, equity, and inclusion. This model invites people into relationship with one another, and healthy relationships provide the foundation for any successful organization."

— Anika Walker-Johnson
Director of Equity & Inclusion, Germantown Academy

"We engaged Christine to assist our Executive Team, a group of experienced, seasoned professionals, to help them problem solve better. Through her curriculum, they went from a team that spoke over one another to a more connected team with better listening skills by using the Listening Path. We would highly recommend Christine Miles and the EQuipt Team to help drive business forward with her listening tools."

— Kelly Sanfedele
Director of Human Resources, Binsky & Snyder

"Christine has provided me tools not only to listen better to my customers, but to connect with them at a new level by allowing them to tell me their story. Through the Story Gathering process taught by Christine, I am able to get past the story at the surface and begin to uncover the real needs, concerns, and challenges that lie below. This has enabled me to provide solutions that truly meet customers' needs as well as gain trust and further the personal relationships that are so important for success in my business. I am very grateful to have been able to work with Christine."

— Lance Yoder
Partner, Director of Professional Services,
Clear Process Solutions

"Christine impacted my world entirely from the moment I first met her. Through consistent personalized questions to truly understand each person she encounters and the depth of genuine compassion she provides in encouraging each of those people's stories, she has not only changed the culture within hundreds of corporations but also changed hundreds of people's perspectives on how to engage and interact daily with other humans. I wake up every morning asking myself, 'How do I want to contribute to the world today?' and I remember my 'why.' Those two sayings cross my mind daily, and it's all because of Christine. I believe that any person reading this book will take away genuine nuggets that will help to fulfill if not transform their day-to-day life."

— Nina Di Francisco
Oregon Regional Director, Member Services,
Info-Tech Research Group

"Christine was a candid and effective speaker. Our group of HR professionals valued her message on the importance of listening, and her delivery via storytelling made her session an engaging and interactive experience. Christine's knowledge, insights, and techniques to improve listening skills are highly relevant and applicable in both personal and professional settings."

— Tanisha Campbell
Event Producer, HRO Today

"Christine Miles is an exceptional executive coach, friend, and supporter. Creating strong, practical communications delivered with humor, humility, and empathy that are designed to help you win are what Christine does best. I highly recommend working with Christine. She has helped me greatly and I have relied on her to help many members of my team. No Bull. Just good stuff."

— Tony Koblish
CEO and President, TELA Bio

"Christine Miles is by far the ultimate expert in helping people and companies achieve their goals. As the HSBC Whistleblower, my listening, understanding, and actions led to the largest fine against a bank in US history. I passed information to the Central Intelligence Agency regarding the bank terrorist and drug cartel financing. I now own a private intelligence agency, Tactical Rabbit, comprised of former CIA field operations officers. Our mission is National Security and my team launches private intelligence operations where the stakes are high and failure is not an option. Christine was brought in as a consultant because of her expertise in not just listening, but identifying what information is important and then converting that potential energy into kinetic understanding. Christine is an expert at listening, understanding, and then *action* to bring about a desired result. My team relied on her critical advice to bring us back to the CIA intelligence methodology roots required for us to get the job done. If you want to know how to unleash the power of listening, this book is a necessity!"

— Everett A. Stern, MBA
Intelligence Director, Tactical Rabbit
US Senate Candidate 2022

"Listening is a skill people need to master to navigate in today's digital world. The ability to truly listen and understand one another is becoming harder as remote work continues to gain popularity. Christine effectively teaches you how to build your unique path of understanding through easy-to-use tools and effective storytelling—all the tools you need to bridge the communication gap, whether you are looking to unlock team performance or grow revenue. I highly recommend this book if you are looking to grow your organization's EQ."

— Milena Schaefer
VP of Planning and Transformation, Apparel Company

"I had the opportunity to have Christine work with my team on how to more effectively show up for their customers. Christine's ability to break down the listening process and give tools to effectively engage with people to gain true understanding is an invaluable skill in business and in life. I am so happy she decided to write this book and share her insight on a broader scale."

— Michael O'Donnell
National Vice President – Utilities,
SAP North America

"I didn't even realize I wasn't listening until I read *What Is It Costing You Not to Listen?* Christine Miles has convinced me I need to be a better listener, and she has given me the tools to do so. I'm learning to be less impatient and to quit thinking about how I'll respond, as well as to ask better questions during my conversations. This book will change your life and your business. It's powerful beyond words."

— Tyler R. Tichelaar, PhD
Award-Winning Author of
Narrow Lives and *The Best Place*

"In *What Is It Costing You Not to Listen?*, Christine Miles shares her hard-earned truths about how little we truly listen to each other. She offers techniques that are realistic and easy-to-use but will take some practice. I encourage you to invest in this book and the processes described. Then listen to the powerful responses you get from people when they realize you are listening."

— Nicole Gabriel, MBA
Former Senior Executive, General Motors
Author of *Finding Your Inner Truth*
and *Stepping Into Your Becoming*

"Christine Miles reveals in these pages what few of us realize. Not only are we not listening, but it's not our fault. No one has taught us how to listen. Now Christine shows us how, in what should be a required college course but is presented simply in this book, the power of truly listening. Her stories, techniques, and down-to-earth teaching style will make you wish you had read this book years ago."

— Patrick Snow, Publishing Coach and
International Bestselling Author of
Creating Your Own Destiny and *The Affluent Entrepreneur*

"Easy to read and impactful, this powerful book is chock-full of valuable advice to manage 'roadblocks' to listening that cost managers time, money, and productivity. The author shares her skills and years of experience to help you learn how to listen with empathy so people feel heard and, more importantly, understood."

— Susan Friedmann, CSP
International Bestselling Author of
Riches in Niches: How to Make it BIG in a small Market

A PROVEN SYSTEM TO GUIDE AND TRANSFORM HOW YOU LISTEN

WHAT IS IT COSTING YOU NOT TO

LISTEN?

THE POWER OF UNDERSTANDING
TO CONNECT,
INFLUENCE,
SOLVE
& SELL

CHRISTINE MILES

AVIVA
PUBLISHING
New York

WHAT IS IT COSTING YOU NOT TO LISTEN?
THE POWER OF UNDERSTANDING TO CONNECT, INFLUENCE, SOLVE & SELL

Copyright © 2021 by Christine Miles. All rights reserved.

Published by:
Aviva Publishing
Lake Placid, NY (518) 523-1320 www.AvivaPubs.com

All Rights Reserved. No part of this book may be used or reproduced in any manner whatsoever without the expressed written permission of the author. Address all inquiries to:

www.EQuipt-People.com

ISBN: 978-1-63618-149-3
Library of Congress Control Number: 2021916614

Editors: Tyler Tichelaar and Larry Alexander, Superior Book Productions
Cover Designer: Nicole Gabriel/AngelDog Productions
Interior Book Layout: Nicole Gabriel/AngelDog Productions
Author Photo: Nemi Stanisic

Every attempt has been made to properly source all quotes.
Printed in the United States of America
First Edition 2 4 6 8 10 12

DEDICATION

To my mother, Susan, whose warmth and thirst to be understood shaped who I am and how I understand.

To my father, Charlie, who raised me to never set limits on what I can achieve.

To Michael, for always supporting me to chase my dreams and prevail through adversity.

To Dean, for coming into my life at the most unexpected time, for your loving heart, being my champion, and seeking to understand me.

To all those who generously give the gift of understanding to others.

To you, the reader, for your desire to listen differently and understand.

"Listening is an attitude of the heart, a genuine desire to be with another, which both attracts and heals."

— *L. J. Isham*

ACKNOWLEDGMENTS

Deb Adams, Bill Artosky, Gary Banks, Justin Barr, Rachel Blumenthal, Hank Boyer, Kyle Bray, Dan Brewer, Katy Bruer, Herb Cohen, Lee Crump, Jeff Dierks, Nina DiFrancisco, Barb DiJohn, Dave DiMaria, Kevin Duffy, Andy Fussner, Richard Garber, Dr. Marion Lindblad-Golberg, Kelly Goldovich, Faith Hawley, Ann Hook, Claus Torp Jensen, Anita Walker-Johnson, Wendy Kleiner, Ken Knickerbocker, Tony Koblish, Linda Kreiser, Kaihan Krippendorff, Dr. Peter Kuriloff, Frank Lacapra, Sue Lehrman, Mika Maloney, Janne Marconi, Katrina McKay, Rhonda McKinley, Carol Miller, Kevin Nally, Dr. Perpetua Neo, Michael O'Donnell, Ginny Palmieri, Mark Ray, Frank Rhea, Jill Robert, Don Rossi, Anita Rowan-Schwartz, Kelly Sanfedele, Milena Schaefer, Alyssa Smith, Everett Stern, Sue Szczepkowski, Rona Taylor, Lance Yoder

SPECIAL THANKS

To Dean Borig for being my sounding board and helping make this book and me better.

To Colleen Duffy for your perspective and being the voice of the reader.

To my team, Elizabeth Thomson, Marv Perel, Matt Broley, Ingalis Salonen, Tarrynn Deavens, Kayla Muscato, Todd Kieling, Sue Vanderoef, Kristen Haldeman, Sarah Good, and Dena Lefkowitz for believing in our mission, sharing your gifts, and helping transform how others listen.

To our client heroes who help shape our story while we help shape theirs.

To Hanlon Creative, Emily Gorka, Drew Hanlon and Chris Hanlon, for bringing my vision and story to life visually.

To Patrick Snow for his brilliance simplifying how to make the dream of writing this book a reality.

To Tyler Tichelaar and Larry Alexander for their amazing editing skills. Without their talent, this book would just be an incomplete Word document on my laptop.

To Nicole Gabriel for the brilliance of her simplicity in the cover and interior design.

To Susan Friedmann for taking me on as an Aviva author.

"*Listening is an act of love. When you listen to people, you are communicating non-verbally that they are important to you.*"

— *Jim George*

CONTENTS

"Listening is often the only thing needed to help someone."

— *Unknown*

THE GIFT OF UNDERSTANDING

*"There is power in understanding the journey of
others to help create your own."*

— *Kobe Bryant*

I believe understanding is one of the greatest gifts we can give and receive in life. I also believe we can fix what is broken in us by giving others what we need for ourselves. Growing up with a mother who felt unseen and misunderstood inevitably gave me the gift of understanding others, but very often, it also left me not feeling seen or understood myself.

I have found that the more I see others, bear witness to their pain and ultimately understand them, the more I heal my own wounds and losses, cultivating both personal and business success. I have spent my life and career helping others learn the emotional skills of connection, understanding, awareness, and listening to drive business outcomes. I learned how to listen and see what was going on beneath the surface, to hear what was not said because of my circumstances starting at the age of five. Most of us are not taught these skills.

A couple of years ago when I was traveling the country speaking, an event coordinator, Faith, commented, "Christine, it must feel so good that everyone likes you." I laughed at her comment because I certainly know not everyone is a Christine fan. Faith saw the many people who came to talk with me after my speech or at the end of the event and how we were engaged in conversation. People would share their very personal stories of success, pain, and passion, pulling back their veil to let me see who they were behind the professional veneer. My genuine interest in understanding who they were and their stories, even for a few short moments, created a powerful experience.

The gift of listening—and listening differently—is transformative for both the person being seen and understood, and the one doing the seeing and understanding. Unfortunately, I believe we are in an epidemic drought of understanding.

I decided to write this book because I believe people want to listen, understand, empathize, and be present for the people they love, care about, and work with, but we have not been taught how. We are all failing at listening while doing very little to address or solve the problem, and it is costing us dearly. We blame people for not listening while we primarily teach people how to talk, know, and tell.

My hope is to create a movement where listening, not speaking, is recognized as the most important and powerful form of communication. Where there is personal focus on developing the skill of listening and where educators, business leaders, and corporations put time and resources toward the cause.

The journey begins with you. I will take you on the path of how to transform how you listen, giving you the gift of understanding, and you will receive more than you gave as a result.

This book is divided into three parts: Section One about why listening is so important; Section Two about how to listen differently; and Section Three on the Listening Path™, which provides the tools you need to transform how you listen.

As someone with dyslexia, who is also fundamentally impatient, I understand we all read, absorb, and learn differently. I have included both written exercises to help you build your skills along the way and summaries to give you snapshots of each chapter. This is your book, your guide, my gift to you to use in whatever way works best for you.

"'I'm listening' solves more problems than 'I'll fix it' ever will."

— Unknown

LISTENING YOUR WAY TO SUCCESS

"Any fool can know. The point is to understand."

— *Albert Einstein*

Are you a good listener? Whatever your answer, according to *Harvard Business Review*, chances are you are rating your listening ability much like your driving skills. You think you are above average or better than you really are.

Have you ever asked yourself how your spouse, children, mother, father, employees, business partner, boss, colleagues, or customers would rate your listening ability? Would your opinion hold up? Oh, if there were only a listening test we had to pass before we hit the road of life, so many major problems and losses could be prevented.

When you make a mistake driving, the consequences are obvious; you have a near miss, an accident, or get a ticket. You are usually aware you messed up, even without grave consequences. When listening on the road of life, your mistakes are usually far less obvious. It's death by 1,000 cuts, where the surface wounds are barely felt until the problem is so big you can't stop the bleeding.

Although listening is regarded as one of the most critical business and life skills, our education system doesn't teach us how to listen. Our ability to listen is treated like our ability to walk—don't worry; it's a natural thing; you'll figure it out…. What? Unfortunately for us, it doesn't work that way.

What is not listening costing you? Have you gone through a breakup, divorce, had employees leave, not made a deal, lost a customer, have children who are struggling, friendships that have been lost, children who you're not close with, a team that can't get things done together? In all these scenarios, the ability to listen is a common thread to both causing and solving these problems. Have you ever asked yourself how your ability to listen affects your life? What have you lost? What are you about to lose? What are you missing without even knowing it?

I feel your pain. It's difficult to solve a problem you don't know exists. How would you know? It's not your fault that you don't know how to listen. It's not your fault you don't know what it means to be a good listener. It's not your fault you don't know what not listening is costing you. It's not your fault you don't know what to do about it.

We live in a world where little time and resources are spent on teaching people how to listen. In fact, we do quite the opposite. We teach people how to tell, to know, and to speak, while listening is the communication skill we need. We spend zero time on listening in our grade school education, and only 2 percent of us have had any type of listening training. Yet, we blame the listener for not knowing how to do it.

In this book, you will learn why listening, not speaking, is the most powerful form of communication. The inability to listen is at the core of so many problems we face, and learning how to listen to understand is a key to good problem solving.

The ability to listen to the stories people are telling themselves about you is the first part of learning to listen differently. Your appearance, your demeanor, makes a difference. People form biases and tell themselves stories when they meet you. They don't know who you are, and you don't know them. By listening first, you will learn how to overcome these stories and tap into others' stories to help influence, lead, solve problems, sell, get things done, and love with understanding.

Great people influence us, and what makes people great is how they make us feel. You will learn that people don't care how great you are; they care about what you went through to become great. You will learn how to listen to yourself to understand your origin, your passion, and your purpose so you can better listen to others.

We live in a world where talking and telling predominantly dominate our communication when, instead, we need to listen and understand. As we communicate and solve problems, too often we assume, "If I tell someone to do something, they will leap into action and just do it." This just doesn't work in relationships, in sales, in business, or in general.

People don't like to be told anything, really—even if they are asking you to tell them; you'll learn not to fall for it. Telling causes resistance, not action. In your effort to be helpful and solve problems, you become part of the problem. The approach is wrong, and causes us to miss a huge opportunity.

The answer is learning to *listen to understand*, uncovering the insight and meaning first. This enables you to change the conversation forever and get things done.

Until now, that was easier said than done. Listening is so hard. The subconscious is a superpower, and it is in charge; it's in control. When you're listening, your subconscious is firing on all cylinders and telling you to do everything, except listen. Your subconscious is your enemy. Attentive listening is the old paradigm of attending to the teller by showing them you are paying attention. With this approach, we tell people what behaviors to exhibit to show they are attending, but we don't give them the tools to know how to do it. A low "I'm paying attention, so I'm listening" bar is set. The old paradigm teaches people how to underachieve.

In this book, you will learn the new, game-changing paradigm for listening and Story Gathering—a transformational approach to listening that allows you to discover the hidden gems in the conversation. You will learn to hear not only what is said but what is not said. By traveling the path, you connect with the teller, find the meaning of the story, and earn the right to help them solve their problem.

You will learn to identify your listening persona and identify exactly when an unhelpful persona shows up. You'll use tools to soothe your subconscious so you can listen differently without having to think about it. The meaning, the message, and the insight of the story will find you.

You will be shown the Listening Path framework, and the five tools you need to transform the way you listen. The path ensures you will not get confused as you listen to a story and gather its meaning. Then it will guide you and the teller to a new beginning or accomplishing a goal, which can be solving a disagreement, aligning with yourself, another, or the world, being more loving, making a sale…you name it.

You will learn how to read the map that guides you on the path. You will learn how direct questions interfere with listening, and how to have more success by using just six questions. These are the questions used by master story gatherers, journalists, and therapists.

You will learn how to *reflect* in a new sense. Traditionally, to reflect is to think deeply and carefully. It is also what a mirror does, showing us who we are. The Listening Path marries the two ideas into the practice of verbally reflecting what you have heard in thirty to ninety seconds so you can sift all the story ingredients, blending the right mix of facts, details, and emotions into your reflection to ensure and demonstrate understanding.

You will learn how understanding and agreement are very different from one another.

You will learn that affirming creates alignment, breaking down walls and silos, sparking creativity, and helping you solve difficult problems.

Finally, on the Listening Path, you will learn how to *mini-reflect* so you and the teller are checking in, following the same footsteps, and speeding up the process of getting to the story without getting lost.

Listening is notoriously hard. The Listening Path was created to make this difficult act simple by virtue of design. If you follow the Listening Path and use the tools offered in this book, your listening skills will be transformed. Story will become your ultimate tool, helping you transform how you listen, show up, understand yourself and others, and develop your emotional intelligence (EQ) and skills along the way. These emotional skills make you great.

Why should you listen to me? I certainly don't profess to have all the answers. Listening has been my passion, my purpose, and my life's mission. My purpose started when I was five, growing up with a mother who suffered from mental illness stemming from the loss of her mother when she was only three months old. My mother was warm, funny, and loving, but underneath the surface she suffered great pain and sadness. My role was to see and understand her pain. I learned early in life to listen differently, hearing, and seeing what wasn't said. The ability to "listen to understand" has been the single thread in all of my successes and has helped me overachieve relative to my average abilities.

I have spent my entire life and career being both a student and teacher of listening. I've been a student of psychology, receiving my undergraduate degree in psychology at Millersville University and my post-graduate degree in psychological services from the University of Pennsylvania. I started my career at twenty-two as a home-based therapist trained by and working with world-renowned therapists in structural family therapy.

I've dedicated my life's work to helping individuals, families, and business leaders elevate how they engage, connect and listen to have greater success. I've traveled the country and many parts of the world learning from others how listening is the universal language of love, connection, and caring. I've succeeded at listening more than I have failed, but I have paid close attention to the failures so I could share them with you.

This book and this map are the culmination of fifty years of studying how to make this complicated skill and powerful form of communication simple to learn. I've devoted my life to learning and teaching others how to "listen to understand."

It's difficult to learn something new, and you may be skeptical that listening can deliver what I'm promising. You might feel apprehensive, thinking you've been you for a long time and "it's hard to teach an old dog new tricks." You might be feeling excited that you can learn to listen differently and improve your relationships, reach your sales goals, and/or stand out as a leader.

Whatever you are feeling, I get you. Success is not an accident. This book provides you with the simple framework and tools you need. You will get halfway to transforming how you listen by learning what the tools are. The rest of the solution lies in using the tools. If you want to get to the meaning of the message faster—improve your proficiency as a listener—you will need to practice the tools.

Not to worry—I am here to take your hand and guide you along the Listening Path to help you both learn and practice your way to success. I will help you stick to the process, and you will become a highly skilled story gatherer. You will completely change your game and your results by learning one new move at a time.

Are you ready to be great? Are you ready to learn how to approach others in a way that makes them feel like they want to connect with you, trust you, and care for you so they will follow, love, buy-into, and believe your message? Listening is an unselfish act, a gift that, given freely, will yield huge returns.

You have endless opportunities to listen differently and practice your way to success. Practice with your children, your spouse, the Uber driver, a stranger, or the cashier at the grocery store. Watch what happens when you take the time to listen differently, even for just a few moments. Practice with your customers, your employees, your boss, your colleagues—and again, watch what happens.

I promise others will feel better interacting with you, and your relationships, business, happiness, and success will be forever transformed.

Let's get started walking this path together.

Christine

*"Instead of talking in the hope that people will listen,
try listening in the hope that people will talk."*

— Mardy Grothe

?

SECTION ONE
LISTENING MATTERS

"One who listens learns; one who learns listens; one who listens and learns is on the path to enlightenment."

— *Matshona Dhliwayo*

?

Chapter 1

FAILING TO LISTEN

*"Life can only be understood backwards
but must be lived forwards."*

— *Soren Kierkegaard*

I distinctly remember the first time somebody asked me what I wanted to be when I grew up. I was about eight years old and riding in the car with my dad and a friend of his. I responded with the utmost certainty, "I want to be a psychologist"; even at my young age, I knew what that meant. Many of us who go into the field of psychology do so to heal the wounds from our childhood. I am no different.

Growing up, I saw my mother's pain from losing her mother at three months old. Other people only saw a woman who on the outside was happy, loving, fun, funny, and connected; they did not see the depths of her pain below the surface. At a very young age, it became my responsibility not only to see, but also understand her pain. While there was great burden in this responsibility, there was also a great gift; I learned to listen differently—that is to listen to understand. This ability to listen differently has been my game-changer and the single thread in any, and all success I have achieved.

How important is listening? How much has your ability to listen or not listen affected your success, both personally or professionally? Are you failing to listen? I want you to be asking yourself these questions all along the journey we are about to take together—the journey to Transformational Listening. My life and career have been devoted to helping people learn to listen differently. Listening differently to themselves, others, their spouses, children, customers, prospects, teammates—you name it.

For decades, I've been doing my own research with friends, family, colleagues, clients, and audiences around the world, asking them "How important is listening?" Here's what I have heard and learned. Listening is universally regarded as one of the most critical business and life skills. Now you would think with such a universal, "it so critical" answer to this question, that the skill of listening would be "top of mind," or at least on the radar as a critical skill that business leaders and people should be devoting time and resources to developing…wouldn't you?

Unfortunately, listening remains a skill that is assumed, rather than learned or taught. The inability to empathetically listen and uncover the real needs of others is costly, but it is no one's fault. We blame the listener while we spend the majority of our resources teaching and training students, leaders, and employees on how to speak, be knowledgeable, and tell.

Failing to listen is merely the result of not being taught how to do so in a simple, yet transformative way. Clearly understanding the message, the messenger, the story, and the expectations; delivering smarter insights; and driving greater value all hinge on your ability to do one fundamental thing…listen differently.

BECAUSE OPRAH SAID IT

Did you know that everyone has a story? It's true. Why do I know this? Well, of course, because Oprah said it. Regardless of your opinion or your like or dislike for Oprah, her words have significant weight with a lot of people, and for good reason. She has an ability to tap into people; to understand them and what they need, what they like, and who they are. Everyone has a story, and stories are important. Stories connect us and help us understand one another. When we listen, we are primarily listening to stories. Like my mother, most of the story lies below the surface and is not seen. When you listen to understand the story, you won't fail; the meaning finds you.

After her long-running daytime talk show ended in 2011, Oprah had a series on OWN (Oprah Winfrey Network) called "Your Life Is a Master Class." Oprah defines a master "as someone who has stepped in and owned the progress of their life. One who knows how to live, to keep going, never quit, rejoice in the good times and in the bad, when their stories help the trajectory of others who will listen."

When you listen to understand the story, you won't fail; the meaning finds you.

I don't profess to have all the answers, but I do know that I have listened carefully and intently for decades. I have been both a student and a teacher to get to this point, to deeply understand the power of listening differently and how to make this very complex skill simple to learn and do. My life has been my master class on the skill of listening to understand.

WHY I DO WHAT I DO

If I had only one word to describe why I do what I do, that word would be "understanding." I believe understanding yourself and others is one of the greatest differentiators to success. When it comes to my natural abilities, I am quite average, and at best, above average in some areas—whether it's academically, athletically, raw intelligence, you name it. Despite being pretty ordinary, I've managed to achieve extraordinary success in some areas of my life.

I have been able to overachieve relative to my ordinary natural abilities, and that overachievement can be attributed to my ability to listen to understand. My ability to listen differently has helped me to navigate academically and overcome my learning challenges, and to get accepted to the University of Pennsylvania to earn my Master's Degree in Psychology. That's another story; I actually sold my way into Penn.... It helped me, an average athlete naturally, become an athlete who made it to the US field hockey trials on two occasions because I understood not only how to read the game, but my opponent.

Listening to understand got me professional opportunities with no previous experience, including my first professional job as a home-based therapist, where I was trained and worked with world-renowned clinicians as well as ran the organizational development arm of an Employee Assistance Program. I was leading the team, designing and delivering customized trainings for our corporate clients at the age of twenty-eight, without having any training or management experience. More than anything, listening has helped me understand myself, my limitations, my strengths to drive myself to a higher level of performance and persevere through obstacles in life. Listening prepared me for the hardest thing of all: at age thirty-one, having almost all of it taken away and having to fight to reinvent myself after suffering a cervical spine injury from a car accident. We all have a story; let me tell you more about where mine started.

TAKING YOU BACK TO THE BEGINNING

My passion for listening started when I was very young, as early as age five. I grew up in Hershey, Pennsylvania, about five miles from Hershey Park. Have you been to Chocolate World or visited the amusement park? Two hands up if it's a yes and you like rollercoasters.

I grew up the youngest of two, surrounded by plenty of open space, lots of room for outdoor play, and lots of friends in the neighborhood—a pretty idyllic childhood by all accounts. But it was far from the pretty picture people saw on the surface.

Despite my mother's outward appearance, she suffered from mental health issues: depression, anxiety, and more. I've often said my mother came by her mental health issues very honestly, both biologically and environmentally.

My grandmother, like my mom, suffered from mental illness. The story goes like this…. My grandmother had rheumatic fever when she was a child. At twenty-eight, the doctors emphatically told her she should not have children because childbirth would further weaken her already weak heart. My grandmother disregarded that advice, and within three months of giving birth to my mom, died.

I can still remember seeing the picture of my grandmother in a wheelchair holding my newborn mom. I don't remember how old

I was when I first saw that image. But I was aware from a young age that my mother carried so much sadness and pain below the surface from this profound loss and being the cause of her mother's death.

Now, a little bit about my dad. My dad instilled in me a love for business. He grew up in Port Royal, Pennsylvania, on a chicken farm not far from Pennsylvania State University. He studied agriculture at Penn State, and when he graduated, he sold chicken feed. In his words, people called him a "chicken shit doctor" because, apparently, what you feed the chickens matters greatly in keeping the chickens healthy.

My dad's early success in sales opened the door to an opportunity to sell for Connecticut General Life Insurance in Philadelphia. At this time, organizations were making huge time and resource investments not only to ensure salespeople were trained to understand their products, but also to truly understand their customers and their needs. By the time I was five, my dad had decided to start his own financial planning practice serving small businesses.

I never saw the chicken farmer my dad once was. I only saw the businessperson, working in his office, telling stories about his clients, their happy times, the tragedies of losing children, illnesses, and their desires for security. It was very intimate. Even as a young person, I could see and feel how much his clients mattered to him—and how much he mattered to them. My dad would tell me you have to know and understand everything about your clients if you truly want to help them achieve what they want. It was business talk, but I could see it was more than that—it was very personal.

I learned to pay attention to what wasn't said, the story below the surface, the intangible, the unseen, by observing both my mother and father. I was never afraid to ask a question about emotions or be curious about what I didn't understand. To me, questioning was normal; it was just what was expected and what I learned early in life.

DISCOVERING MY GIFT

As early as high school, I realized my intangible skills were helping me in unexpected ways. At the end of my senior year, I received an invitation for the senior awards banquet. The invitation did not identify which award I would be receiving. I was completely perplexed. I went through every category of awards I could think of to see what I might possibly be receiving. I knew for sure I wasn't getting the math, science, English, or music award. I ruled out the best athlete award—that was going to my friend Lynn, who was more deserving.

As I sat in the auditorium on the night of the award ceremony, they called my name, "Christine Telfer (my maiden name) is the recipient of the Good Citizenship Award." Who knew the Good Citizenship Award even existed?

Here's why receiving that award was so significant and why it's so interesting to me. In hindsight, I wasn't the student who raised money for charities or did public service. I didn't do anything notable or extraordinary to be a good citizen. The only thing I did was make it a point to understand people from different groups. I tried to understand those who looked different from everyone else in the class.

For example, I had two albino classmates and a classmate afflicted with cerebral palsy. These three students were picked on relentlessly. I was so amazed by the grace with which they handled themselves in the midst of the adversity they faced. I would intervene when I could, but mostly, what I did was ask about them and how they were doing. I got to know who they were and connected with them.

I believe I was recognized for my curiosity and insatiable desire to understand them and my other classmates and teachers. That I sought to understand and see others was what my teachers saw as being a good citizen.

The awards ceremony was when I began to understand how having these intangible skills could help me achieve in ways that hadn't occurred to me. This started me on a life and career path based on leveraging these gifts. Through my life's work, I have come to understand that I was different because I learned how to listen differently. Most people were not taught this skill that I learned early.

WHERE WE ARE GOING

What are your gifts? My desire, my passion, and my purpose is to help you transform how you listen so you can achieve a new level of success you didn't even know was possible. I want to help you make your gifts even more powerful by tapping into a skill, *listening,* that you may not have put a lot of purposeful time or attention into developing. Many articles and books have been written about the importance of listening and how to be a better listener. However, most focus on what to do, not how to do it in a simple, applicable way.

I have intentionally written this book to be your guide to learning to *listen to understand*. I'm taking your hand, taking you on the path to understanding why, how, and what you need to do to transform how you listen. Listening to understand is not something we are taught. I will show you what you need to do, and in a simple way, so you will actually be able to do it.

THE PATH TO TRANSFORMATIONAL LISTENING

Listening is more than hearing something or even helping someone feel heard. Listening differently goes beyond being empathetic to truly understanding another's experience, understanding them and their story, and really seeing them—hearing not only what is said, but also what is not said, seeing what is not only on the surface, but what lies below the surface. When you tap into this ability, it transforms everything—your results, your relationships, your business, and yourself. The ability to listen differently transforms how you show up, lead, sell, influence, and succeed in every aspect of life. Helping people transform how they listen is my purpose, my passion, and my mission, and it is the heart of why I do what I do.

Transformational Listening is a breakthrough approach that goes far beyond traditional, attentive listening. It is far superior to attentive listening, which focuses on "paying attention" to the teller differently by making eye contact, being present, etc., telling the listener what to do, but not *how* to do it. The human brain is the enemy of our ability to listen. The attentive listener is essentially "white knuckling" as they fight their subconscious to stay present during a conversation. This internal struggle leads to missing both the message and the messenger, causing conflict, misalignment, and missed opportunities.

The framework I developed, called The Listening Path, provides the critical tools needed to calm the listener's subconscious so they can not only attend but hear both what is and what is not being said. This shift from attentive listening to Transformational Listening, also referred to as Story Gathering, will enable you to uncover underlying problems, gain trust, earn credibility, and consistently provide smarter solutions, forever changing the conversation.

EXERCISE

List three areas of life you want to change by transforming how you listen.

_____

_____

_____

CHAPTER SUMMARY

1. Listening, not talking, is the most powerful communication skill and is regarded as one of the most critical business and life skills.

2. More time and resources are spent teaching people to tell, talk, and know than to listen.

3. Failing to listen is merely the result of not being taught how to do so in a simple, yet transformative way. Clearly understanding the message, the teller, the story, and the expec-

tations, and delivering smarter insights and creating value, all hinge on your ability to do one fundamental thing…listen differently.

4. Everyone has a story, and stories are important. Stories connect us and help us understand one another. When we listen, we primarily listen to stories.

5. Listening differently goes beyond being empathetic. It includes hearing not only what is said but what is not said and uncovering the insights.

6. Transformational Listening, or Story Gathering, is a breakthrough approach that goes far beyond traditional, attentive listening. Attentive listening focuses on "attending" to the teller differently, telling the listener what to do, but not "how" to do it.

7. In this book, you will journey down a path to understanding why, how, and what you need to do to transform how you listen.

?

Chapter 2

MEASURING THE COST OF NOT LISTENING

"One who fails to listen, fails to learn."

— Unknown

'**ve** spent my life and career asking people the question: Is listening important? I usually get the same answer—listening is critical, yet little to no attention is paid to developing it.

Listening is a skill we assume people have, rather than need to learn. Most of our time and resources are spent teaching people how to tell, talk, and know rather than how to listen. I believe the paradigm of what is important is upside down. Listening is the most powerful communication skill, not talking. The ability to understand that everyone has a story, and that more is going on below the surface, is critical. These are things I learned to pay attention to.

> **Listening is the most powerful communication skill, not talking.**

This ability has been the single thread to any success I've had. I've come to realize that listening to understand is not something most people learned as I did. I have a deep passion for helping others gain the ability to listen to understand. It's why I do what I do. In this book, we are setting out on a path together that will guide you in transforming how you listen.

YOU CAN'T SOLVE A PROBLEM YOU DON'T SEE

Let's start on the path by understanding what it costs not to listen. Why is so little attention being paid to developing the ability to listen when it is such a critical skill? Have you considered what it costs? Have you noticed? Are you aware of the costs of not listening?

Everyone has a story, and most of the story lies below the surface. The same is true for listening—most of the difference listening can make is invisible, lying below the surface. Listening or not listening influences every human interaction and relationship and has benefits or consequences, respectively. The consequences of not listening are vast, yet ironically, can go unnoticed and unseen, all while damage is being done.

Listening is something we just assume people are doing—we take it for granted. Because someone can hear, we assume they can listen. Listening and hearing are two different things. Let's compare listening to seeing.

Many of us assume people who can see can also see colors. However, an estimated 250 million people in the world are color blind; that is, they can't distinguish colors. We take it for granted that all people who can see can also distinguish that the sky is blue; we assume. Hearing is the ability to perceive sound. By contrast, listening is the ability to understand the message. We assume if one hears, one is listening.

We don't have a term for listening blindness—that is, blind to the message or the meaning. Because listening is assumed, it's a problem that goes unnoticed. When we don't notice or see a problem, it's unlikely we are going to do something about it. Basically, we can't fix what we are not aware of.

Like many salespeople, I was guilty of expecting my potential clients to fix a problem they didn't know existed. I would start with the solution for helping their people listen differently, rather than first ensuring they understood the problem. I took the wrong approach and ended up blaming them for not understanding the value of listening, which meant I wasn't helping them see what was below the surface. I assumed my prospects could see color.

To solve a problem, you need to see the problem and think about what it costs you. Again, what does not listening cost? Is it hurting your personal life—your relationships with your spouse, partner, children, friends? What is not listening costing you in your professional life?

EXERCISE

Write down three costs of *not* listening personally or professionally.

_____

_____

_____

MAKING IT A MISSION

As the world changes incredibly quickly, I have seen failing to listen become a massive problem, and the associated costs are also getting bigger and bigger. The more I focus on the problem of not listening, the more I understand listening helps solve most problems.

In 2018, I had an epiphany. I realized it was time to make it my mission to help the world see once and for all that we need to put attention, time, and resources into the problem of failing to listen. I found it is my mission to help as many people as possible by showing them the tools they need to transform how they listen.

My first step in the process was forming my business, EQuipt, with the purpose of equipping people with the emotional and human skills to help them be more successful. Our core focus is transforming how people show up and how they listen. Then, starting in early 2019, I spent a year traveling the country giving keynote addresses at chief information officer (CIO) forums. During this time, I developed a better understanding of how technology leaders saw the problem of not listening. In turn, I was also able to help these leaders see there is a better way to make digital transformation successful in their organizations. A digital transformation is the integration of digital technology into all areas of a business, fundamentally changing how you operate and deliver value to customers. It's also a cultural change that requires organizations to continually challenge the status quo, experiment, and get comfortable with failure.

I started by doing more research so I could spread more awareness of the need to listen properly. Then, in each city, I once again started with that all-important question to the audience of self-proclaimed left-brained thinkers. "Raise your hand if you believe listening is important." Regardless of the city, the age of the executive, or the years of experience, every hand immediately went up. "Yes, listening is important."

The more I focus on the problem of not listening, the more I understand listening helps solve most problems.

Then I'd ask, "Why is listening important?" Again, the answers were universal. Save time, avoid making decisions based on incorrect or inaccurate information, deliver optimal solutions, create a climate of engagement, spend less, and so on.

Then I would ask, "What about personally? What is not listening costing you in your personal life?" The answers: divorce, conflict with my spouse or my partner, disconnection from my children, relationships suffer, etc.

As I reflected the audience's answers back to them, I asked, "Why aren't you devoting resources to help your teams learn how to listen differently?"

After ten cities and asking thousands of CIOs, I found most agreed listening was vital, yet few had clear answers as to why more wasn't being done to close the gap between knowing listening is such a critical skill and the need to do something about developing it. To say it was frustrating is an understatement.

FAILING TO LISTEN IS NO ONE'S FAULT

Did you know that in our thirteen years of education in the United States we have zero education on listening? Or did you know in business we use listening 40 to 80 percent of the time? Did you know the higher your position in an organization, the more important listening becomes to making good decisions? If you have only part of the story and the wrong information, you make bad decisions.

Listening Training

Time utilized at work vs. formal education
of the average employee

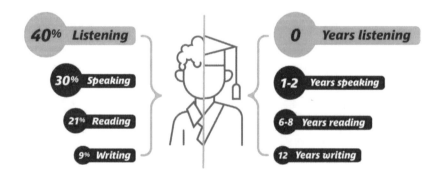

40% Listening	0 Years listening
30% Speaking	1-2 Years speaking
21% Reading	6-8 Years reading
9% Writing	12 Years writing

By contrast, the previous graphic shows that we spend more time both at work and during our educational years reading and speaking than listening (source unknown). Obviously, the pyramid is upside down, and yet we're not doing anything about it.

MY LISTENING FAILURE

In 1987, after graduating from Millersville University with a degree in psychology, I started looking for my first professional job in Lancaster, Pennsylvania, where I was living. I was offered a sales job, which, ironically, I turned down because I didn't want to go into sales. Instead, I took a position where, at twenty-two, with no professional experience, I was going to people's homes saying, "Hello, I'm Christine. I will be your family therapist."

I have never done more selling than I did in that job. I was selling myself as a therapist, selling help for families in making changes, and selling to help families open up and be vulnerable.

Fortunately, one benefit of the job was having a world-renowned structural family therapist from the Philadelphia Child Guidance Center teach us how to sell to families and help change how they functioned. These clinicians would come to our offices regularly or we would go to Philadelphia to meet with them.

One of the first families I worked with was a mother, father, and their eleven-year-old son, their only child. The son had been psychiatrically hospitalized for a few months and had just returned home. Structural family therapy focuses on helping the family system function better as a unit, rather than viewing the child as the problem. The father was rather stoic and emotionally disengaged from his son. It was clear the boy was angry that his father was so emotionally remote, and he was acting out to get attention. Having no experience, I was at a loss how to get the father to engage differently with his son.

I did what I thought I was supposed to do—I went to my boss for help. My boss, Ed, was a social worker, but he had never done family therapy of this kind. In hindsight, he was in over his head and didn't know how to help. Nevertheless, Ed jumped in and told me exactly what I needed to do.

Ed told me in the next session I was to tell the father exactly what I had just told him. Ed said, "Tell the father he is totally disconnected from his son, and that is why his son is acting out—to get attention."

I thought, *I can't say that to the father; the indirect message is that it's the father's fault that the son is in crisis.* I pushed back on Ed's advice, and then the suggestion became a directive. I was to do exactly what Ed instructed me to do: explain the family dynamics to the father in front of the son and mother, and then come back and report to him what happened.

I felt incredibly nervous sitting in the family's living room and uncomfortable thinking about what I was to say. However, like a good employee, I did exactly as I was directed. Surprisingly, I managed to say what Ed had told me to say and got through the session. The family didn't say much, but there was no major disaster as I had expected. What happened next I did not see coming.

The next day, not only did the father call the agency I worked for, but he also called the referring agency, Children and Youth, requesting a meeting to discuss my actions and try to get me fired. A meeting was called with my boss' boss, two people from Children and Youth, my boss Ed, and the mother and father—all to discuss me. I was not permitted to be in the meeting, so the discussion went forward without me present to defend myself. Unfortunately, Ed didn't have the courage to confess that I was following his directive, and let me take all the blame. I was barred from further contact with the family, but fortunately, I didn't lose my job.

The experience was incredibly painful for so many obvious reasons, but there was a hidden gift. I learned that the cost of not listening and telling is very high. By telling, I lost credibility, trust, and my reputation—and I could have lost my job. Telling the dad wasn't the answer; even if what I had told him was true, it wasn't a helpful approach.

I realize now that telling is all Ed knew how to do, so he told me to tell. Listening to understand the father would have been a much better approach. Obviously, more was going on below the surface that we needed to uncover. I believe if I would have listened to understand what it was like to have a son who had been hospitalized for three months, to see his son acting out, and to see his son in pain, I would have gained the father's trust. Then, and only then, could we shift to telling the father what he needed to do differently. I also learned a valuable lesson on the importance of listening to myself rather than following orders.

EXERCISE

Write down an experience when you told instead of listened. Include what it cost you.

_____

_____

_____

_____

THE UNDERDEVELOPED SKILL

Have you been taught how to listen or taken a course on listening? Ironically, even once we enter the business world, very little attention is paid to developing listening skills. Statistically, only 2 percent of people have had any kind of listening training (*Progressives Listening Facts You Never Knew*). I'm the perfect example. I am a certified family therapist with a master's in psychology. Certainly, I've had a course or two in listening? Nope. My training came from my early life, as you now know.

In the home-based program where I worked, I was recognized for what the clinicians thought was my innate ability to listen; in reality, I had been trained to listen differently from the age of five. When I started to research the problem of most people being so underdeveloped in their ability to listen, I saw how staggering the gap was between expectation and actual training. I realized that to solve the problem, we needed to develop a better way to teach and give people the tools to know how to listen. I set out to develop the framework to close the gap.

THE COST OF NOT LEARNING HOW TO LISTEN

Now let's go a little deeper into what *not* listening is costing us in business. Did you know that customers don't expect their salesperson to be able to help them solve their challenges? According to *Buyer Insight*, a study conducted by Forrestor found that "only 13 percent of customers believe salespeople can demonstrate an understanding of their business challenges and how to solve them?"

Would it surprise you that according to Web Strategies "74 percent of buyers said they were more likely to buy if salespeople would simply listen to them, and that 95 percent of buyers state that the typical salesperson talks too much."

These are just a few statistics about the high-level problem of how listening impedes the ability to sell. When I share these statistics, I usually hear, "That's why I tell my salespeople 'We have two ears and one mouth for a reason.'" While I appreciate the sentiment, telling someone to listen twice as much as they talk is easy; helping them do so takes much more effort. Telling people to listen doesn't solve the problem when they don't know how to listen differently.

WHAT IS IT COSTING YOU NOT TO LISTEN?

Let's go back to those discussions with the CIOs in 2019. I was working with an organization called Premier Connects. Premier was the pioneer in creating forums for chief information officers, bringing CIOs together to learn about technologies that could support digital transformation in their respective organizations. Eighteen years prior, when Premier was founded, information about current technologies was harder to come by. I was introduced to the leaders at Premier Connects, President Nina Di-Francisco and the new CEO and Owner, Alisa Smith, who knew they were at a critical juncture in making their events more relevant.

Technology leaders needed to gain insight beyond understanding the technology available. They needed innovative approaches to the human capital within organizations. The CIOs themselves talked about how the people aspect of the business was the linchpin to digital transformation success, and much harder to figure out than the technology.

Premier Connects listened and was looking for ways to make their events more people-centered. I got involved to help them fulfill their vision, so we partnered in 2019 to shift the paradigm. I gave two keynote addresses at the events; the opening address was on how you present yourself as a leader. (I will talk more about this in Chapter 8 when I share my purpose story.) The closing keynote address was on how to listen differently.

Early on in our year-long travels, we were in Atlanta, Georgia. I met Lee Crump, the CIO of Rollins at the time, an approximately eight-billion-dollar organization. Back then, Crump was regarded as the mayor of the Atlanta CIO network. He became part of my opening address where I interviewed him on stage to get his backstory. I called him after the event to get his feedback on the event and his experience.

Crump said:

> Christine, what you did in the keynote about how people show up was magnificent, and very impactful. What you did in the afternoon on listening, that is game-changing. I can speak for those of us in the technology world; we really don't know how to listen.
>
> First of all, we hire really smart people who have tremendous skills building technical solutions. However, these same people are not wired naturally or taught to ask the right questions to uncover the real need of our customers; they are problem solvers who rush to the solution. The result is that too often we deliver what is asked for instead of what is actually needed. This is a very costly endeavor as rearchitecting solutions are actually more expensive than the initial implementation. We lose time and credibility with our key stakeholders and customers. We are problem solvers, not listeners, and without the ability to uncover the real issues, we will never deliver what is really needed. We will always miss. What you shared shows us how to fix the problem.

Crump's feedback was just what I needed to hear to confirm I was on the right mission. The costs of *not* listening are enormous; plus, we are not addressing the problem, and we are blaming the listener when it's not their fault.

WE ARE THE PROBLEM

Technology organizations implementing digital transformations are only one aspect of the business that is affected by the cost of *not* listening. Technology leaders are not the only ones who don't know the problem exists or are not doing anything about it. Has anyone ever been frustrated with you for not listening, but you thought, *I am listening*? We get frustrated that our employees, salespeople, IT professionals, customer service professionals, etc. are not listening. Why are we surprised that people don't know how to listen when we are only teaching them how to know our products, our process—to know and to tell?

Our teams are following our guidance and doing what we've asked them to do. We haven't identified and addressed the problem or given them the training to know how to listen, to ask the right questions to uncover the real need.

> **Why are we surprised that people don't know how to listen when we are only teaching them how to know our products, our process—to know and to tell**

Your frustration is real; I get you. To put it bluntly, you've been providing the wrong solution to the listening problem by teaching your teams to tell.

Now that you know the listening problem exists and very little time and attention is paid to developing the skill, are you more inclined to spend time learning how to listen differently? Are you more inclined to ensure your team has the tools they need to listen effectively?

EXERCISE

Write down three instances when not listening affected you negatively in your personal or work life.

_____

_____

_____

CHAPTER SUMMARY

1. Have you considered what not listening costs you? Have
    you considered the damage of not listening to your life,
    your relationships, and your business?

2. The consequences of not listening are vast, yet they can
    easily go unnoticed. Not listening causes problems that
    are like death by 1,000 cuts. The small wounds aren't felt
    until it's too late. Relationships are damaged or lost, em-
    ployees leave, you lose a sale, etc.

3. The more we've focused on the problem of listening, the
    more problems we realize listening solves.

4. We blame the listener for failing when we've spent zero
    time in school on listening. Furthermore, only 2 percent of
    people have had any kind of listening training.

5. Buyers say that the typical salesperson talks too much,
    and they would be more likely to buy if the salesperson
    would just listen.

6. The inability to listen to uncover the real business need results in delivering what the customer asks for instead of what they need.

7. Like color blindness, we have "listening blindness"—we hear sounds but can't distinguish the meaning of the message.

8. We all fail at listening. Telling people to listen does not solve the problem when they don't know how to listen differently.

?

- Chapter 3 -

SOLVING THE WRONG PROBLEM

"A problem well stated is a problem half solved."

— *John Dewey*

The cost of not listening is so big and vast that it is difficult to quantify and measure. Listening and not listening intangibly touch everything we do in our business and personal lives. Since little time, attention, or resources are given to building listening skills, it's not surprising most people aren't aware of the costs of not listening and why it's a problem they're not trying to solve.

The problem is like color blindness—we see but can't distinguish color. With listening blindness, we hear sounds, but can't distinguish the meaning of the message. The result of not listening is death by 1,000 cuts. We barely feel the surface wounds until the problem is so big we can't stop the bleeding.

Frankly, the more I focus on helping people learn to listen, the more I realize how many problems listening actually solves. Not listening is at the core of so many problems we face, and listening to understand is at the core of good problem-solving.

Have you ever considered you might be solving the wrong problem? That you might be fixing something that doesn't need to be fixed? Answering something that isn't being asked?

ARE YOU IN SALES?

In the last chapter, we looked at some statistics about what not listening cost salespeople. We talked about how not listening leaves customers feeling like the salesperson does not understand their real challenges and how to solve them. How helpful would it be if the salesperson just listened more?

Not listening is at the core of so many problems we face, and listening to understand is at the core of good problem-solving.

My question for you is: Are you in sales? Even if you're not, these statistics will also pertain to you.

Many people see sales as a little bit of a dirty word. We don't like to feel sold to because we think we are being pressured or the reason someone is selling is simply for their own gain. Selling is also about convincing someone of something. For example, when you describe the reason your department should be allotted certain resources rather than those resources going to another part of the business, you are "selling."

Zig Ziglar said, "We are all in sales." This is something many of us have known intellectually for a long time, but when I ask people if they are in sales, they are still reluctant to own the title. In

Chapter 2, I mentioned that I didn't want to go into sales, and although I held positions that included selling, I denied I was a salesperson for most of my career. I'm sure I did a lot of selling in my personal life that I am unaware of as well, but looking back, my first big sale happened when I applied to graduate school. Let me take you back.

After spending two years working at the in-home program, I knew it was time to increase my professional knowledge and earn my master's in psychology. I decided to take a big swing and apply to the University of Pennsylvania. I wish I could say I had some noble reason for wanting to go to Penn; the primary reason was acquiring the gravitas and credibility of having a degree from an Ivy League school. I struggled with math and science, so my SAT scores were lackluster to say the least. If the field hockey coach hadn't been selling me to Millersville University, I would have never been accepted. I learned about ten years ago that I am dyslexic, and I never felt like I was academically smart enough. To me, graduating from Penn meant people would automatically conclude I was smart.

Not surprisingly, my GRE scores were just as deplorable as my SAT scores. I certainly didn't meet the criteria or standards to get into Penn, but I decided to apply anyway. I thought my work experience and letters of recommendation from high-profile people next door at the Hospital of the University of Pennsylvania would likely get my application a look, and they did.

I got an interview with the chair of the psychology program, Dr. Peter Kuriloff. I remember walking into his office and having a very nice conversation with him and thinking it was going pretty well. I'll never forget what he said at the end of my interview: "You're not going to make it here, Christine. I'm sorry. The answer is no."

I was so disappointed. Especially after being on campus, I wanted to go to Penn for more than just the credibility—I had fallen in the love with the school and the program. I wanted it more than ever but I thought, *That was that—Penn is a no-go.*

I went home to my parents' house, sat in the kitchen, and told my father what had happened. My dad said, "Why are you giving up? You need to convince Dr. Kuriloff you can make it at Penn. Why don't you write him a letter? Tell him what it would mean for you to go to Penn and that you can do it."

I'll never forget my father's exact words: "Tell Dr. Kuriloff it is your fervent desire to go to Penn and be part of his program, and you will do whatever it takes to be successful."

I followed my father's advice to a tee, and within a couple of months, I got a letter telling me I was on the waiting list. I was ultimately accepted for the following fall. There is no doubt that my Penn education has served me well over the years in so many ways, including that people assume I'm smart by just looking at my resume. I've said many times that I sold my way into Penn, thanks to my dad's help. Getting into Penn was my first big sale.

Most of us sell in ways that are more about influence than getting someone to buy a product or service. Sales is how we get others to opt in to our vision, our ideas—it's how we build credibility and/or put forth our point of view. In my case, I sold to Dr. Kuriloff.

Dr. Kuriloff's surface concern was that, based on my scores, I didn't have the academic chops to make it at Penn. His underlying issue was he didn't know if I had the drive to overcome my academic deficiencies to make it at Penn. My dad saw the real problem and helped me craft the right message to allay Dr. Kuriloff's concerns, convincing him I would not allow myself to fail.

Have you ever considered that you are selling in your personal life, not just your business life? Whenever you give your spouse advice, try to tell your child about the dangers of distracted driving, or explain why they should do their homework, you are selling. Selling is part of life. The more we accept that we need to sell, the more efficient and effective we will be.

When we sell well, we create better outcomes for those we want to help and those we care about, and we help ourselves. Selling is offering advice, services, or products to be helpful to a loved one, a colleague, or a customer. Problem solving is at the root of sales, and most of us are selling to be genuinely helpful and help solve a problem.

EXERCISE

Describe a recent moment when you were selling, either in your personal or business life. Did you make the sale?

_____

_____

_____

ITS NOT ABOUT THE NAIL

As we bring solutions to others, we have a tendency to start solving or fixing the wrong problem. I found a great video called *It's Not About the Nail*. I show it in workshops to make the point about solving the wrong problem. It starts out with a close-up shot of a woman saying, "It's all this pressure that feels like it is right up in my forehead, and it's relentless, and I feel like it's never going to stop." The camera pans back, and the woman turns to her boyfriend—and we see she has a nail in her forehead.

The woman's boyfriend understandably says, "Well, you know you have a nail in your forehead, and if you just took that nail out then...." She interrupts with, "Stop trying to fix it. You always do this." He responds, "No, I'm not trying to fix it. I just think if you took the nail out of your forehead...." Again, she interrupts him, telling him he doesn't understand, and the exchange goes on in a similar fashion with more comedic misses back and forth. Eventually, he looks at her and says, "This must be really hard for you." Finally, she responds with, "Thank you," and we feel her relief at being understood.

I won't spoil the final shot for you, but it ends rather humorously. Most people's reaction to the video is they can relate and have had a very similar conversation with a spouse or partner—the whole men are from Mars, women are from Venus story. Then I change it up by asking those in the workshop, "How many times have you had this kind of conversation in business?" They answer, "Quite frequently."

EXERCISE

Think back to the last two weeks and write down two examples of when you either offered a solution or got one before listening. How did it make you feel?

_____

_____

_____

_____

SELLING TOO SOON

Whether we're aware of it or not, we often sell too soon. Understanding is the precursor to solving any issue. What happens when we try to sell too soon is similar to what happened with the couple and the nail in the forehead. While we may see the problem very clearly, the person experiencing the problem may not see it at all. Ready for more bad news? The more you know, the more you tend to rush to provide a solution.

Information, knowledge, and experience can actually be the enemy of listening and understanding. Instead of helping our partner, children, or customer feel understood, we go right to the sale— let me tell you what's wrong and how to fix it. However, you haven't earned the right to sell. Not yet. Think about it—our curiosity goes down as our experience and knowledge goes up.

Not too long ago, I was on a call with a team of engineers from Greece, the VP of Sales of their North American distributor, and their customer. They were discussing validating the results of an energy savings project they had implemented. The results were quite compelling: they are saving the customer a guaranteed 10.6 percent annually in electricity costs, which was a huge return on investment (ROI). The purpose of the call was to help the customer, Dan, understand how the engineers arrived at the 10.6 percent validated savings.

As soon as the call started, the Greek engineering team shared their screen on Zoom. What I saw was a beautiful diagram with all the calculations validating the results. However, I didn't understand the math or statistics or how they arrived at their conclusions. While it was a PowerPoint work of art, they jumped right into the numbers and solving the problem without asking any questions of the customer. As I listened and watched, the drama increased, and Dan, as the customer, became more and more frustrated.

This went on for about ten minutes before the VP of sales asked everyone to pause. He said, "Dan, you understand these results, but you actually need to be able to explain them on a seventh-grade level so you can easily explain them to your bosses. You want to get their buy-in, so they'll want to do more projects in the future...do I get you, Dan?"

Dan responded, totally relieved, with an emphatic yes, and the conversation changed completely. Everyone got on the same page, working to solve the actual problem rather than assuming they knew what the problem was.

In the end, Dan, the customer, was trying to ensure he could be an effective champion and salesperson within his organization for the technology. He understood the results were correctly validated, but he didn't know how to explain them at a seventh-grade level. This opportunity would have been completely lost if the VP of sales had not paused to listen differently, understand, and uncover the real need.

Everyone had good intentions, everyone wanted to help the customer, but their intentions did not match the effect. This is often the case in conversations. Do you ever find yourself advising or problem-solving before clarifying or understanding? Do you find yourself feeling frustrated when people offer you advice or a solution when you haven't asked for it? What happens then?

NOBODY LIKES TO BE TOLD WHAT TO DO

From a psychological standpoint, I have understood a basic human principle for a very long time. It seems kind of obvious when I say it out loud, but many of us don't consciously think about the consequences of doing it. We are in a world of talkers and tellers. For some reason, we believe that telling someone to do something will lead them to act. Nothing is farther from the truth. Are you ready for the truth? Hold onto your hats—here goes: Nobody likes to be told what to do.

We are in a world of talkers and tellers. For some reason, we believe that telling someone to do something will lead them to act.

I learned this lesson the hard way when

I began working as a counselor at an employee assistance program (EAP). Having started my career as a therapist at twenty-two, by thirty I had a lot of experience. Nevertheless, I put my Penn diploma on the wall so clients would see I had credentials behind my advice. When I saw a client for the first time, I asked how they would like me to help them. The response was usually the same. "I'd like you to help me solve my problem. You are the expert. I'm looking for your advice and for you to tell me what you think I should do."

I fell for it, hook, line, and sinker. I would listen, understand the problem the best I could, and because I had a lot of experience seeing the same problem, quickly move to telling my client what to do, just as they asked me to do.

Not surprisingly, I was immediately met with resistance and all the reasons they couldn't do what I was suggesting. I know now this is a common sales trap. The customer asks you to tell them how to solve their problem so they can tell you why they can't do what you tell them. If you don't see the trap, you will fall for it, advise too soon, and lose the sale. It's not a conscious process on the customer's part, but rather a subconscious one.

It's human nature to respond, "Don't tell me. I won't listen." The right to give advice or solve the problem needs to be earned so the defenses come down, and people become willing to listen and act.

How many times have you gotten caught in this trap with a customer, teenager, or friend? They're looking for the answer; you have it, and you are happy to provide it. But in the end, you often feel like trying to help was a complete waste of time.

SLOWING DOWN TO SPEED UP

It's not just human nature not to like to be told what to do; it's also human nature to believe that telling someone what to do is the fastest way to make progress. Go figure? Telling someone what to do creates resistance. The reality is when you create resistance, you slow things down; you impede progress. One of the core principles behind listening differently and listening to understand is the power of slowing down to speed up. It's counterintuitive, and therefore, hard to put into practice, but if you follow this principle, it really does change so much.

When I was in grad school at Penn, I was also an assistant field hockey coach. Having played as an undergrad at a division three school, I was thrilled to be coaching division one athletes. The athletes were stellar, and many of them were incredibly fast, particularly the forwards. As a field hockey player, I was not known for being the fastest—my stick work defined my game. As a defender, the ability to outsmart the faster athletes who were used to running at full speed down the field was key to my success. I told the athletes if they ran at one speed, they might beat me down the field a couple of times, but I'd figure out how to get them most of the time by taking the right angle to cut them off and by anticipating their next move. However, if they took a hitch step—a sudden momentary stop—broke their pace, and then sped up again, they'd force me to stop, and I wouldn't be able to read or anticipate what they were going to do next. This would make it difficult to catch them, and they would beat me most of the time.

Think about the times when you have slowed down just a little bit to think about your next move, where you needed to go, or took a step back—what happened?

We tend to run down the field at full speed and forget to pause—simply slowing down is a powerful tool for getting where you are going faster.

Good problem-solving requires us to slow down to speed up. Taking a hitch step to ensure we are listening to understand the person and the problem earns us the right to solve it.

Good problem-solving requires us to slow down to speed up. Taking a hitch step to ensure we are listening to understand the person and the problem earns us the right to solve it.

When we are selling and problem solving, the tendency is to rush to the solution, to tell, and then we solve the wrong problem or don't solve the problem at all.

EXERCISE

Write down three examples of when you rushed to solve a problem. What did that cost you?

_____

_____

_____

CHAPTER SUMMARY

1. Not listening is at the core of so many problems. Listening to understand is at the core of good problem-solving.

2. When we offer to help solve a problem, the solution might seem obvious to us, but it is not obvious to the person with the problem.

3. We all sell. Selling is how we get someone to opt in to our vision, our ideas, and it is how we build credibility and/or get our point of view across.

4. Problem solving is at the root of sales. We sell too soon by rushing to solve the problem before we have earned the trust and the right to solve a problem.

5. Having an abundance of information, knowledge, and experience hinders listening and understanding. The more you know, the more likely you are to rush to the solution and tell people what you think they should do.

6. It is a basic human principle that no one likes to be told what to do. Yet we live in a world of talkers and tellers and believe that telling someone to do something will lead them to act.

7. We rush to solve the problem before listening to understand.

8. Sometimes the one rushing to solve the problem is the buyer. This is a common sales trap—the buyer asks you to tell them the solution and then rejects you for doing so.

9. Slowing down to speed up is a helpful principle for getting to the solution faster. Slow down, listen, connect, and understand first; then the person is more open to you helping them solve the problem.

?

- Chapter 4 -

UNCOVERING HOW STORY IS THE ENGINE OF EQ

"In the past, jobs were about muscle, now they are about the brains, but in the future, they'll be about the heart."

— Minouche Shafik, Director of London School of Economics

Much of what we do involves solving problems. We are all in sales because the heart of selling is problem solving. You have a problem; I have a solution. Let me convince you that my solution to your problem is the one you should choose. Unfortunately, our underdeveloped ability to listen to understand often leads us either to solve the wrong problem or not solve the problem at all.

In my experience, most people sell to be helpful. I have found few sell for their own gain. Like with the nail in the forehead, we see someone in pain and want to tell them to take the nail out. But telling them what to do, even when it is completely obvious, doesn't work. Why? Human nature. We don't like to be told what to do, so telling actually leads to resistance.

We rush to selling to solve the problem before listening to understand first. Taking a step back, slowing down to understand, actually gets to the solution faster.

UNDERSTANDING THE IMPORTANCE OF EQ

Learning to slow down and listen to understand is one of the soft skills, also known as emotional skills. Do you know what it means to have emotional intelligence? Emotional intelligence (otherwise known as emotional quotient or EQ) is the ability to understand, use, and manage your own emotions in positive ways to relieve stress, communicate effectively, empathize with others, overcome challenges, and defuse conflict.

I often hear people equating EQ with having good people skills. While this is accurate, I believe the deeper meaning of EQ is one's ability to understand emotions: both others' and our own. How many of us are skilled in understanding and addressing our emotions or others' emotions? Are we skilled in doing this in business?

I can't tell you how many times I've heard someone say asking about emotions or feelings in a business conversation is way too personal and none of their business. As I said above, I've been curious about and asking about people's feelings since I was a little girl, so I am undaunted by asking, and I have seen the power of simply doing so.

I find people's hesitation to ask or seek to understand feelings in business both fascinating and perplexing. The reality is that humans (people) make up all businesses. People feel, so if we do not tap into our and others' emotions, we miss the point. But don't take my word for it.

WHAT MAKES THE GREAT ONES GREAT?

Have you ever worked with or known someone who is absolutely great at what they do? Well, of course you have. But why are they great? What are they doing that other people are not doing?

EXERCISE

Please take a moment to think about a boss, mentor, coach, leader, or someone you've worked with. Write down three qualities, behaviors, or characteristics that made the person you are thinking of great.

What did you come up with? What do these characteristics or qualities have in common? What is the theme? My team and I have been asking what makes the great ones great everywhere we go in the world, whether virtually or in-person for over a decade now. We've asked CEOs, salespeople, leaders, engineers, teachers, lawyers, women, men, millennials, Zs, traditionalists, Gen X-ers, baby boomers…you get the point. Regardless of the demographic, nationality, race, gender, etc., the answer is always the same. The majority of the qualities and behaviors listed involve emotional skills—the great ones listen; they communicate effectively; and they are authentic, caring, and more. Rarely do we hear them described as the smartest in the room, the person with the most product knowledge, and/or the most experience.

The person described as great is someone who makes others feel a certain way. Maya Angelou said, "I've learned that people will forget what you said, people will forget what you did, but people will never forget how you made them feel."

What makes the

great ones great?

Empathic

Humble

Open

Sense of humor

Trustworthy

Committed

Good Communicator

Listens

Gets people to want to
follow

Charismatic

Transparent

Flexible

Passionate

Cares about people

Has a vision

Resilient

Walks the talk

Honest

Driven

Vulnerable

We are all human, and we are all led by our emotions. When we are surrounded by people who know how to make us feel good about working with or for them, more gets done. Understanding your emotions, and the emotions of others, is critical to success in all aspects of life. Listening differently is a fundamental skill for understanding emotions and building emotional intelligence.

UNDERSTANDING YOURSELF FIRST

I have devoted my career to helping people develop their emotional intelligence. Over the years, I believe I have helped many individuals, families, leaders, teams, and businesses. My approach to helping others build their emotional intelligence is similar to building a house. First, you need to build a solid foundation. If the foundation isn't solid, the house is going to have problems over time, and there will be cracks and issues that will continually arise.

Listening is the foundation of every aspect of emotional intelligence. Let's start with listening to yourself. Daniel Goleman, in his book *Working with Emotional Intelligence*, calls self-awareness the "inner rudder." Goleman defines self-awareness as the ability to recognize and understand personal moods, emotions, and drives. Simply put, self-awareness is understanding your moods and your thoughts about your moods. At the core of understanding your emotions, and yourself, is your ability to listen.

Do you understand yourself, your story, and how it has shaped your life?

Uncovering, listening, and understanding your own story is the path to self-awareness and greater emotional intelligence.

Uncovering, listening, and understanding your own story is the path to self-aware- ness and greater emotional intelligence.

I was in New York about six years ago working with a digital marketing compa- ny. I worked with a sales and marketing team on how to listen differently and tell customer stories (we call them custom- er hero stories; you will learn about this concept in Chapter 21). After I opened our conversation by telling them why I do what I do, a young woman in her mid-twenties approached me and told me her story. She said she related to the story of my mother because her mother also suffered from psychological prob- lems. She said, "My mother has two personality disorders." Then she added, "You are much more forgiving of your mother than I am of mine."

I looked at her and understood the pain she felt not having had a mother who could provide her the security and stability she needed as a child. I could see this young woman hadn't yet fig- ured out all her emotions and how her backstory influenced her life. I appreciated that she was searching, and I appreciated her courage in being so open and vulnerable with me.

I replied:

Well, I figured out that my mother came by her problems honestly. My grandmother had psychological issues, and my mother experienced early childhood trauma and loss, so she was set up both biologically and environmentally. This understanding of my mother's story and her emotions helped me better understand myself, my own feelings, and reshape how I navigate my own life more effectively. I didn't want to become a victim, but rather a reasonably healthy survivor, so understanding all the emotions was part of surviving and thriving. Listening to yourself and understanding your own story first helps you become more self-aware.

To this day, I think about that young woman and hope my story in some way helped shape hers for the better.

WHAT VERSUS WHY VERSUS HOW

Do you understand why you do the things you do? The why is the heart of emotional intelligence. In 2010, Simon Sinek did a groundbreaking Ted talk called "What Great Leaders Do to Inspire." If you haven't seen it, it's about twenty minutes long and well worth your time. It was groundbreaking because his message was based on neuroscience and *how* people believe. Simon asks, "Why does one company succeed while another company fails?"

Simon says success is not simply about having a superior product, but how the company differentiates itself and gets others to buy in. In a nutshell, most people think mainly about what they do instead of why they do it. Why the people running a company believe what they believe is much more powerful, as is how people who buy think. If you don't know what someone believes, you can't know whether you believe in them. The human brain is wired emotionally and wants to hear why before what. Think about a five-year-old—their curiosity is off the charts and they're constantly asking why. We may not articulate this question as often as a five-year-old, but our subconscious is also constantly looking for the why, not the what.

What does all this have to do with emotional intelligence? If we understand why we believe what we believe, tap into our emotions and the emotions of others, and communicate that why, we are inherently more effective.

Over the past decade, I've witnessed how business leaders have begun to see the importance of emotional intelligence.

I'm on the board of advisors of a local college just outside of Philadelphia, the Rohrer College of Business. About two years ago, we had a meeting where we were asked for ideas about how to get the students business-ready and what programs were needed. As I sat at the table with my breakout group, one gentleman spoke up. "I can teach new employees what they need to know about my business. The much harder thing is to find talent with a higher EQ."

The other business leaders followed suite, agreeing that when they hire people with these human skills, more often than not they become the most valuable employees in their organizations. While this was music to my ears, unfortunately, we are still not doing enough academically or in business environments to teach or promote EQ.

While business leaders agree emotional intelligence is important, a gap still exists between seeing the need and teaching the skills.

Remember, we are in a culture of telling and providing information. Emotional intelligence development training often centers around assessing one's level of EQ, defining EQ, and then focusing on areas to develop. It takes arduous exercises and work to move the needle. Most people don't have the inclination to do this level of work, and results often come too slowly.

Fortunately, I am highly impatient. As an athlete, I was proficient at mastering skills well beyond my scope. I've leveraged this ability over the years to help others learn and build their skills faster and more efficiently, including developing EQ.

I learned the power of "the how to do it lesson" for the first time when I was in college. I mentioned that I was not the fastest athlete. I'm built like my father, tall with rather long legs and a long running stride. In college, my teammates teased me as we watched game films. If I had to run to catch someone, it took a while for my feet to catch up with my stride. Sometimes it actually looked like the video was playing in slow motion when it wasn't. I've often joked I was last one to be first to the ball.

I spent the summer between my junior and senior year living at college. One night, I went out with my friend Deb from the track team to do sprints to get ready for pre-season. I don't know what I was thinking. We went out on the football field and set up on the end line. Deb looked at me and said, "We're going to do twenty-five-yard sprints. On the count of three we will go. One, two, three...."

I looked up, and before I had taken three steps, Deb was already at the twenty-five-yard line. She turned to me and said, "Christine, you don't know how to run."

I thought, *What are you talking about? I know I'm not the fastest, but I certainly know how to run.* This was the late '80s. Technical running drills and skill building were not a common practice for division three athletes. Running quickly—being fast—was an assumed skill.

Deb said, "Let me show you how to run differently." We set up on the end line again, and this time she showed me how to place my hand, how to position my starting leg, how to place my elbow, and my fingers. It was specific, nuanced, and visual. Within a few tries at implementing her techniques, I got faster.

Next, I practiced what Deb showed me until it became automatic. While I still wasn't the fastest athlete on the field, in one evening of being shown how, I dramatically improved my speed. Sometimes we make things much more difficult than they have to be. Let's keep it simple.

EXERCISE

Write down an example of when you were taught how to improve a skill.

_____

_____

WHY STORY

How do we build our emotional skills efficiently and naturally? How can we go out on the field and, with a few techniques, improve our ability immediately? I show my clients a video on what versus why. It's the musical version, if you will, of the Simon Sinek Ted talk. It's called "Breaktime with Michael Jr., Know Your Why." Here's how it goes.

Comedian Michael Jr. hosts a live event and has a segment called Break Time where he asks a random audience member a question. In this particular video, he spoke to an audience member, Darryl, a music teacher. Michael said, "So you're a music teacher...can you sing?" After Darryl confirms he can sing, Michael prompts Darryl to sing a few bars of "Amazing Grace." Darryl proceeds to sing...his singing is competent, in tune, and good, but it's not compelling or memorable.

Then Michael tells Darryl he wants him to try a different version and gives Darryl the backstory. This time Darryl sings "Amazing Grace" in a completely different way and on a completely different level. He's passionate, emotional, connected to the music, and inspiring. The audience is with him, standing up, cheering, and coming along with Darryl on the journey.

What's the difference? The first time Darryl sings, he is singing alone; the second time he's singing both for and with the audience—a shared experience—and he's making people feel something.

As our audience watches the video, my team is watching them. A mirroring process happens—what's happening in the video happens live in the room. As a behaviorist, it is so fun to watch it unfold. As Darryl sings the second time, you can feel the energy shift, the passion change; the inspiration goes up a level in the video *and* in the room.

When the video ends, we ask the audience what they saw and what they noticed. What was the difference between the first time Darryl sang and the second?

The audience quickly gets to this insight...the first time Darryl knew what he was doing; the second time he knew why he was doing it.

Then we ask the million-dollar question: How did Darryl know the why? It usually takes a few responses before we get to the insight. It's so simple, you see, almost too obvious. Unfortunately, too often we are looking for complex answers and solutions when the best ones are simple and obvious.

What was the difference? You'll have to attend.... Just kidding. The answer is, Michael, the host, gave Darryl, the singer, the *story* to sing to.

Developing your EQ is like me learning to run faster. You need the right tools and techniques. Here's the good news: Story is that tool. It only took ten seconds of a backstory for Darryl to transform how he sang—to sing with passion, purpose, and feeling. The tool that got him to sing differently was knowing the story he was to sing.

Giving people the why, like Simon Sinek describes, helps people tap into their passion, what they believe in. These are emotional skills. Listening to your story, the story of others, and understanding the path and map of a story, are the tools that enable you to build EQ without arduous self-help and reflection exercises.

EQ IS THE BY-PRODUCT

Does learning something difficult to learn make you want to try harder or give up? Difficult things can be made simple to learn, and hard things can be fun to learn with the right approach.

In addition to being kind of slow as an athlete, I also didn't like to run. Running always felt like work. I joke frequently that I'm similar to a dog in that if you throw a ball, I will be happy to chase it all day. If you ask me to go out for a run, all I will think about is how long I have to go before I'm done.

I was fortunate to have two incredible coaches in my athletic career. The first was my high school coach Linda Kreiser, a former USA field hockey player and a hall of fame athlete from Millersville, Pennsylvania. They retired her jersey, she was so prolific at Millersville. My college coach, Carol Miller, was also a former USA field hockey player and hall of famer from Delaware University. Both Linda and Carol had an ability to understand what motivated and made their athletes tick.

One thing they knew very well about me was that running alone was not fun and not the best way to motivate me to get in my best shape. Whenever possible, both Linda and Carol made sure they got me in shape with chasing-the-ball drills, rather than just running. They made everything a game so I would be distracted from the actual running part. As I was chasing the ball, running was a by-product and getting in great shape was the result.

While EQ, listening, and building emotional skills are comfortable territory and a lot of fun for me, I am acutely aware that building the EQ muscle and skills are not everyone's cup of tea. Like running, it can be arduous, tiring, a little daunting at times, and feel like work. It's important to make building EQ fun and simple, without arduous, intense emotional exercises. Developing EQ should be done how my coaches approached getting me in shape. Chase this ball, let the story tool do the work, and before you know it, you're becoming more emotionally intelligent without thinking about it.

EXERCISE

Write down what you believe are your two most developed emotional skills.

_____

_____

Write down two emotional skills you would like to improve.

_____

_____

CHAPTER SUMMARY

1. Understanding yourself and others is one of the greatest factors in being successful. Listening differently is a fundamental

skill for understanding emotions and building emotional intelligence.

2. Emotional intelligence, EQ, is the ability to understand, use, and manage your own emotions in a positive way.

3. Many of us are not socialized to be curious, think, or ask about feelings and emotions.

4. When we asked people what makes someone great, the answers reflected behaviors consistent with well-developed emotional skills.

5. Transforming how you listen starts with how you listen to understand yourself. Uncovering, listening, and understanding your own story is the path to self-awareness and greater emotional intelligence.

6. When you know why you do what you do and which story to sing to, you can tap into passion and purpose. This inspires others to believe in and follow you. Lead with the *why*.

7. The human brain is wired emotionally. Tap into people's emotions to get them to opt in.

8. Building emotional intelligence can feel daunting and overwhelming. We at EQuipt have made building EQ a simple and fun process.

?

Chapter 5

BECOMING AN EXPERT IN EMPATHY

*"If you want to get something done,
become an expert in empathy."*

— *Chris Voss*

EQ, emotional intelligence, is an important skill to have in the workplace and at home. EQ is the ability to understand, use, and manage your own emotions in positive ways. In the last decade, business leaders have come to recognize EQ's importance and what it can do for organizations. However, a big gap still exists between knowing why we need to do something and learning *how* to do it. I don't believe we have even begun to scratch the surface in creating movement on *how* to help more people develop their emotional intelligence.

Emotional intelligence needs to be made simpler to develop. The linchpin to making EQ development less complicated and arduous is to use story. Let story be the tool that enables you to be more passionate and understanding to connect and listen on a whole different level.

I learned from the CIOs I worked with in 2019 that technology has significantly changed how we do things, but they also said, fundamentally, technology hasn't really changed anything. Meaning, to get things done, we need people to do them. People are at the center of all business. Building our emotional acuity helps us get things done. We need to be empathetic to our customers, our employees, and those we interact with at work.

For someone like me who's been in the business of empathizing my whole life, the renewed focus on empathy is like receiving a Hallmark card. It is music to my ears that this has become a theme and hot topic. However, knowing that we need to be empathetic and knowing *how* to become more empathetic are two vastly different things.

LEARNING HOW MUCH EMPATHY MATTERS

Let me take you back to a time when things in my life turned suddenly. I was twenty-eight, and after five years of working as a therapist, I made the difficult transition from a traditional psychology job to a job in a business, working for an employee assistance program. This was my dream come true because an enormous opportunity existed for me to quickly get involved in organizational development work and training for our corporate clients instead of just providing counseling.

One day, about a month into my new job, I was on my way to work—it was 8:30 a.m.—when my car was hit head on. The driver was passed out and slumped over the wheel. He actually hit me and didn't wake up initially. I realize that sounds fairly dramatic, but at the time it seemed very benign. I got out of my car and, other than being shaken up, I was fine—I went to the hospital just to be safe.

What developed over the next few days and weeks was another story. My world started to change dramatically. I began to develop chronic and unrelenting pain in my scapula and arm. I struggled to figure out what was causing the pain and to resolve it for about three-and-a-half years. I continued to play competitive field hockey, playing through the pain out of stubbornness and my love of the sport. I couldn't fathom giving it up. However, I was unable to do anything overhead, like shoot a basketball, play tennis, and so much more.

Despite my physical struggles and limitations, I was playing some good hockey, and when I was thirty, I was invited to try out for the USA field hockey team for the second time. At this point, it was like getting invited to spring baseball training, an honor and a privilege to be among the top sixty players in the United States, but a far cry from actually making the team, which consists of the top sixteen players.

Six months later, my chronic pain became acute. One morning during a doctor visit, I went into the bathroom and came out unable to pull up my shorts. I was in so much pain. The tears streamed down my face uncontrollably. In that moment, my life as I knew it was forever changed. I started the ten-year journey of identifying my very complicated problem and finding a level of normal and manageable function again. Up until that point, I had always identified myself as being on the go, an athlete, a career person, chasing the next goal and accomplishment. I was suddenly thrust into a world where movement caused pain, and I had to reorient my entire life.

Time takes on a different meaning when you're in the kind of pain I was experiencing. The world moves slowly. The experience is extremely difficult to say the least.

As I said, struggle, if you allow it, can teach you great things. Trust me. While I couldn't see it at the time, here's what I eventually learned. My pain was intangible, hard to see, and therefore, difficult to understand. People told me I looked fine, even great, all while I was at a pain level of seven to ten most days. I came to realize I was living a version of my mother's story. My mother looked fine, even great on the surface, but she lived at a pain level of seven to ten psychologically. I was just living it physically.

Empathizing is part of what we need to do to listen differently, but it's only part of how we transform how we listen.

While my friends, family, and those who loved and cared about me tried to understand and were incredibly supportive, it was very difficult for them to empathize with what they had never experienced and couldn't see. I became more aware than ever that most people are not taught to see and understand what goes on below the surface.

Empathizing is something we need to pay more attention to doing. Being able to put ourselves in another's shoes and feel what they feel doesn't comes naturally for everyone.

Empathizing is part of what we need to do to listen differently, but it's only part of how we transform how we listen.

My personal experience of people struggling to truly empathize and witness my story only made me more determined to help people *listen to understand*.

EXERCISE

Think about when someone struggled to empathize with something you were going through. Write down what happened and how it made you feel.

_____

_____

_____

_____

GETTING THINGS DONE WITH EMPATHY

Are you thinking, *I don't know how to be more empathetic? How do I learn to empathize more?* Not to worry; as you learn the tools on the path to Transformational Listening, the empathy will come to you. It's a by-product of listening differently. Before we go there, let's talk about what empathy can do for you.

Chris Voss, a former FBI negotiator, wrote the book *Never Split the Difference*. If you haven't heard of or read his book, you may have seen him in the Master Class series. When Chris joined the FBI, he basically flipped the way they went about hostage negotiations. His book's title is based on the idea that during hostage negotiations, you can't simply say, "You know we should compromise; I'll take a hostage, you take a hostage, and we'll call it a day." You, as the hostage negotiator, need to get out with everything. The old way of hostage negotiation was to control and tell the hostage-taker the way it was going to be. Chris's way was to understand, know, and empathize to get to a resolution.

This paradigm shift was not initially welcomed because it didn't make sense to the old regime—until they saw how it effective it was. In the book, Chris says, "If you want to get things done, become an expert in empathy." We can always equate empathy with results. As I learned early in my career when I was negotiating with families who were terribly stuck, empathizing first was essential for getting them to change.

Empathy is defined as the "ability to understand and share the feelings of another." Notice it says nothing about whether you agree or have felt the same feelings. That's a notable distinction. Empathy is about understanding and being able to imagine what it must feel like. This is where we have to listen to ourselves first.

When you avoid the pain, you miss the opportunity to empathize, be present for the other person, and show how much you care about them. This is why I say frequently, "Listening differently is simple but not always easy." We sometimes have to stretch ourselves, force ourselves to be uncomfortable, to get to the result.

MIRROR NEURONS

The reason empathy gets things done is rooted in neuroscience. Most of us have heard the expression "Monkey see, monkey do." The brain has something called mirror neurons. Studies have been done where electrodes were put on two monkeys to connect their brain waves to one another. What they found was that one monkey's behavior and emotions were mirrored by the other. Mirror neurons are a type of brain cell that respond equally when we perform an action and when we witness someone else performing the same action. Researchers haven't yet been able to prove that humans have individual mirror neurons like monkeys, although they have shown that humans have a more general mirror system.

Have you ever walked down the hall at work and seen two people deep in conversation, standing with the same posture, folding their arms the same way, head tipped to one side the same way? One is the mirror image of the other. This is the process of mirror neurons. The two people are joining emotionally by physically mirroring each other. Empathy is a process of mirroring. It's powerful. When I allow myself to understand and feel what you feel, even if I've never experienced it, I'm connecting with you on a very primal and limbic (emotional) level. This is the beginning of earning the right to provide a solution, to challenge, and to sell. By contrast, when I'm not showing empathy, my brain is not connected and more likely to reject, argue, or disagree with you.

UNDERSTANDING SELLS

As we discussed in Chapter 1, the one word I use to describe myself is *understanding*. To understand, first you need to understand the feelings and empathize—actually feel what the other person feels.

When you feel what someone else feels, they are much more likely to listen to you.

Let's return to when I was a therapist at twenty-two in the home-based program. Fortunately, we were partnered in teams of two. My partner, Sue, was thirty-five and had worked as a social worker for the Children and Youth agency prior to working in the in-home program. In her previous position, Sue had the authority to pick up youth who had run away from home and return them or take them to a safe facility. In the in-home program, we had absolutely no authority or power. We only had the ability to influence, not control.

> **When you feel what someone else feels, they are much more likely to listen to you.**

One day we went to do a family session with a mother and daughter. When we arrived, the mother told us the daughter had run away. The mother did not know where her daughter was, but she thought she might be at a friend's house. Sue was the lead therapist so she decided we should go see if the daughter was where the mother thought she might be. We got in the car and headed to the friend's house.

We drove way out in the country to the house. When we got there, we saw the daughter with her friend sitting on the front porch. Sue walked up to the house to talk with the daughter about why she ran away. I followed closely behind, watching things unfold like I was watching a movie. Simultaneously, a woman came out of the house who was clearly the homeowner and mother to the daughter's friend. The mother, in a rather discontented tone, asked Sue who we were and why we were there.

Sue, from years of experience, quickly went into authority mode. She told the mother we had the right to be there and return the daughter to her mother. In my head, I thought, *I'm pretty sure that's not true.* Nevertheless, the exchange went on, and things began to escalate between Sue and the woman.

As the argument got louder, several young, strong-looking men came out of the house and surrounded the woman like a queen bee.

I continued to watch the scene unfold, still thinking we really didn't have any right to be there, and realizing I also would be upset if I were this woman. I saw that this bad situation could easily get a lot worse at any moment, so I decided to press pause. I said to the woman, "I'm sorry. We really don't have any right to be here. This is your home. You don't know us. We just showed up here. It must be confusing and very upsetting."

I could see the woman immediately start to calm down. The young men backed off and went back into the house. Then I asked the woman if it would be all right if we told the daughter's mother she was there and okay. To which she responded, "Of course." I thanked her for allowing us to see that the daughter was okay, apologized again for our intrusion, and we left.

IMAGINING YOUR WAY INTO ANOTHER'S SHOES

I was just a kid from Hershey. I had no formal training, and certainly no experiences where I had faced anything like that situation before. Fortunately, my instinct was to empathize, and doing so allowed us to leave without incident.

Imagine we are out on the football field about to run sprints—let me help you learn to run faster, to be more empathetic. Instead of trying to feel what the other person feels, let's try to imagine.

1. Imagine you are the woman and two strangers show up.
2. Imagine the story you would be telling yourself if you were her.
3. Imagine how you would be feeling if you were her.
4. Imagine telling the story from her perspective.

I was able to show the woman quite clearly that I understood because I was able to put language to the feelings she was not expressing just by imagining I was her for a few moments.

Do you see how you can imagine your way to stepping into someone else's shoes without experiencing what they have experienced?

EXERCISE

Think of a friend who is going through a difficult time. Write down how you imagine they may be feeling as outlined above.

_____

_____

_____

_____

Empathy is about heightening your emotional acuity. Practice imagining being in someone's shoes. It's okay if it's not automatic for you. By imagining and using story as a vehicle to get into another's shoes, you will become more empathetic. As you learn the Listening Path tools later in the book, you will see that the tools combined with the steps we just outlined will build this emotional capability quite naturally.

CHAPTER SUMMARY

1. If you want to get something done, become an expert in empathy.

2. Empathizing is part of what we need to do to listen differently. Learning to be more empathetic is only part of how we transform how we listen.

3. Knowing that we need to be empathetic and knowing *how* to become more empathetic are vastly different things.

4. Empathy is defined as the ability to understand and share another's feelings. You can imagine your way to a higher level of empathy. Imagine you are the person; imagine you are in their situation.

5. Being more empathetic is not always easy. Others' feelings and emotions can make us uncomfortable. It can be difficult to listen when they are in pain, or when we can't fix the problem. The solution is to bear witness to their pain.

6. Empathy is a powerful mirroring process. You connect on an emotional level when you allow yourself to understand what others are feeling even if you have never experienced it.

7. Understanding sells. When you *listen to understand* someone, they are much more likely to listen to what you have to say.

?

- Chapter 6 -

BUYING, THE SCIENCE BEHIND IT

"When dealing with people, remember you are not dealing with creatures of logic, but creatures of emotion."

— Dale Carnegie

I f you want to get something done, become an expert in empathy. People tend to think that listening and empathy are synonymous. In fact, being empathetic is part of listening well, but listening and empathy are not the same thing. Listening in the transformative way requires more than just being empathetic. That said, empathy is certainly the foundation of listening differently. If you can't understand how someone feels, it's difficult to understand their story and discover insights or hidden gems in the conversation.

Most of us can empathize, but we do it at different levels, depending on our nature and how much we have focused on developing our empathetic ability.

It can be challenging to step into someone's shoes and feel what they feel. Our imagination allows us to follow in another's footsteps. Imagine being that person—what story might they be telling themselves, and how might they feel? Our imagination is the gateway to a greater level of empathy.

Understanding why empathy makes a difference is also important. When we know the why, it's easier to do the how and what. This is an example of slowing down to speed up or doing that hitch step, and changing the pace at which you run to get there faster.

Similarly, *understanding how* people act makes us more effective at influencing others and helping solve their problems.

HOW PEOPLE ACT

Have you ever asked yourself how people decide to buy or act? Have you wondered how people go about making decisions, such as whether to follow someone's advice, buy products, or purchase services? What about in your personal life? Have you thought about how tension builds with your partner, friends, or children? Where is the disconnect between what they want you to do and your willingness to do it?

Psychologists have identified how people make decisions, act, or buy into a new idea in a similar way for decades. It's called the *Events, Feelings, Actions Cycle*. Let me break it down for you.

An event happens; for example, a salesperson approaches a customer. A feeling is evoked—I like this person or I don't like this person—and an action, or more often, an inaction results.

In another example, you see someone walking toward you on a dark street. That's the event. You feel frightened. That's the feeling. You look for somewhere safe. That's the action. That makes sense, right?

Understanding the Events, Feelings, Action Cycle is the basis of cognitive behavioral therapy (CBT). Understanding your feelings and thoughts enables you to control your behaviors. I'm all for that.

In 1991, functional magnetic resonance imaging (FMRI) was invented, enabling scientists to study the brain in real time. What they discovered is that the emotional brain lights up when we decide to buy or act. The decision is emotional, not logical, as we once believed.

Recently, we've found a missing link in the Events, Feeling, Action Cycle. We've found that not only does everyone have a story, but everyone is always telling themselves a story.

Let's go back to walking on that dark street. You're alone at night. You see someone walking toward you. As soon as that happens, your subconscious becomes a storyteller. One story your brain might tell you is this person might mug me. That story informs your feelings—you become frightened. You act because you want to find a safer place.

The story informs our feelings. The story can be based in reality or simply be a perception. Regardless, we need to understand the story first because the story ultimately informs our actions.

SUBCONSCIOUS BIAS

Have you ever had a situation where you didn't listen to the story your subconscious told you and someone, you or another, ended up getting hurt? Logic talks you out of instinctual emotions. The human brain has two parts. Imagine an iceberg floating in the North Atlantic. The part you see above the water is the conscious brain, the logical brain, the thinking brain. But just like an iceberg, what lies above the surface is small compared to what lies below.

The part of the iceberg below the surface is substantially larger and more dangerous—it's a beast, a superpower. That hidden force is our subconscious. It's where all our emotions and stories reside. Understanding what lives in our subconscious, the story we tell ourselves, is essential to self-awareness. When we understand the stories in our subconscious, we get insight into our moods (feelings), and our thoughts about our moods—in other words, self-awareness. Building emotional intelligence is the process of creating awareness of our story and then developing language to describe logically what exists emotionally in the subconscious. This is how we bring the story we tell ourselves into our awareness or above the water.

Gaining an understanding of the story we tell ourselves is why learning to listen to ourselves first is so important.

And to understand others, we must realize they are also always telling themselves a story. Like our own stories, these stories can be based on reality or simply on our perceptions.

Let's go back to the salesperson walking into the room. The customer decides whether they like the salesperson or not almost instantly. It only takes seven seconds for a perception to begin forming.

Why is that? We don't know the person yet. However, most of us don't like to be sold to, so the instant story that comes to the customer's mind may be: "Salespeople are only in it for themselves, for their own financial gain. They'll sell me anything, even if I don't need it, if it means making money for themselves." This story we tell ourselves, our bias, affects how we see the salesperson without knowing them. We tell ourselves stories based on our experience, upbringing, and other similar events. It is up to us to understand where our biases and the stories we tell ourselves come from so we can rise above the subconscious stories that drive our beliefs and behaviors.

Building your emotional acuity and intelligence requires listening differently to the stories we tell ourselves about others. A note of caution—what goes on in the subconscious isn't always pretty.

Building your emotional acuity and intelligence requires listening differently to the stories we tell ourselves about others. A note of caution—what goes on in the subconscious isn't always pretty.

We all have opinions, biases, and thoughts rooted in early experiences and messages. The problem is the subconscious doesn't distinguish between fact and fiction. It can generalize one experience and apply it to all situations.

After my divorce, I rented a home for the first time in twenty-five years. The rental home was a great place in a wonderful neighborhood. I was excited to be there and have a new beginning. My landlord was a man around my age and of Indian descent. Unfortunately, shortly after I moved in, I began to have issues in the house that the landlord was unwilling to fix. It led to a lot of conflict, and I got to the point where I fixed the problems and deducted the cost from the rent. It got pretty contentious. He threatened to evict me, even though I was operating within my rights and on the advice of people in the real estate business.

Sadly, a bias, a story we hear far too often exists. It tells us that, culturally, Indian men don't respect woman and are cheap. Caution: I'm not at all proud of what I am going to admit. Here goes. I fell hook, line, and sinker for this story in the midst of the drama with my landlord. My subconscious said, "My landlord is Indian. Of course, he doesn't respect me; I'm a woman. And he refused to pay for the repairs because he's cheap." The story I told myself was based on a stereotype and bias. This story led me to form what's called a *confirmation bias*.

Confirmation bias is defined as "the tendency to interpret new evidence as confirmation of an existing belief or theory." The bias was Indian men are disrespectful to women and cheap. My landlord was both, confirming that all Indian landlords bully women and are cheap. The original story and bias was confirmed. This story, of course, is far from the truth, but after this experience, my subconscious doesn't distinguish.

It's my responsibility to be aware of my bias and not base my opinion of Indian men on my singular experience. My experience wasn't with Indian men in general. It was with one particular human male. I must listen well to the story I tell myself and understand what is real and what was planted in my subconscious. I must remain aware of that story and shift my subconscious story to focus on what is above the water, realizing my bias is unfair. We must look at people as individuals and not apply one story to all.

Have you ever considered your biases? Have you looked at the stories you tell yourself? What about the stories others are telling themselves?

CHANGE IS HARD

What do our biases have to do with listening? We tell ourselves a lot of stories. These stories create biases that can interfere with how we listen, essentially contaminating the story we are gathering.

The subconscious controls the conversation more than we realize—it can be the enemy of listening.

How do you feel about change? Do you like change? Another story our subconscious tells us controls our perception of change. Change is hard, even for those of us who say they like change. We are creatures of habit. We are comfortable with the familiar.

Many conversations throughout our days involve asking people to change without us even clearly realizing that is what we are asking them to do.

For example, we are asking an employee to change when we talk with them

The subconscious controls the conversation more than we realize—it can be the enemy of listening.

about aligning with common goals and objectives and how to get there. As a leader, you share the vision of where the company is going and what you will need employees to do to help get it there. Another example is a conversation with a customer to help them see how your product or service can solve their problem. What's hidden in all these conversations is that, in order to align, we are asking people to change in some way. We are asking them to change their behavior, their perspective, their actions, or their understanding.

EXERCISE

Write down two reasons people don't like change.

_____

_____

Anthropologists have been studying change for centuries. For example, why do passengers on a sinking boat wait until the last possible minute to get off the ship? This is not just the tale of the *Titanic*. We see this in modern-day stories as well. Do you know the answer? When we ask this question of our clients, their answers range from, "It's comfortable on the boat" and "It's scary in the water" to "People are too lazy to get off the boat," and so on. The actual answer is that people fear the unknown. Generally, people are more comfortable staying with the status quo, even if it's not logical or in their best interests, rather than face the unknown. I know what's on the boat; I don't know what's in the water.

I've shared this story often throughout my career because it makes this very point.

When I was about thirty-four, I ended up in a local hospital with a secondary infection while dealing with the worst of my cervical spine issues. It's funny—we expect to run into someone we know at the grocery store, but not at ten o'clock at night while pacing the hallways and pushing an IV stand in the local hospital; seeing someone I knew was the last thing I expected then.

As I was walking the halls, I looked up and saw a woman walking toward me. She was shorter in stature and had a bandana on her head to hide that she had lost hair. As we approached each other, neither of us looking our best or most familiar, we realized we knew each other. I had counseled this woman, Mika, through a family tragedy a few years prior. We were both shocked to see each other and decided to go back to her hospital room to share our stories.

Mika was only a few years older than me and clearly had undergone chemo. She told me she had discovered a tumor that turned out to be rectal cancer, stage three. It was serious. She was facing a choice between risking surgery that could leave her permanently disabled or trying to eradicate the cancer with chemo. The doctors offered no guarantees either way.

Mika then asked me what my story was. I told her about my accident, how things turned from chronic to acute, and the surgeries I had been through to that point.

Mika is empathetic and always curious about others, which I appreciate about her. Even though I was once her therapist,

Mika looked at me and said, "I'm so sorry for what you've been through. I'm so thankful I'm not dealing with what you're dealing with."

Mika's response actually took my breath away for a moment. I had to call upon my therapy training to muster the courage to say what I wanted to say to get a better understanding of her statement. I said, "With all due respect, Mika, what I have sucks; it's life-changing, but it's not life-threatening. What you have could take your life."

In that moment, Mika taught me a very powerful lesson. She said, "Yes, but I know what I'm dealing with. I don't know what you're dealing with, and I don't want to know." That's how hard facing the unknown is. That's what makes changes so hard. Most of the time we would rather deal with what we know than what we don't know.

EVERYONE TELLS THEMSELVES A STORY

How hard is change for you? What story do you tell yourself when someone asks you to change? We often assume others are telling themselves the same story we are telling ourselves. For example, you're a CIO who is going to implement a new digital process. It's going to make things a lot easier for everyone. That's your story as the CIO, but what's their story? What are the end-users telling themselves? Their story might be very different. They might be saying, "I don't want to learn a new process. You might think it's better, but it's just going to slow me down, and my work backlog is going to pile up."

Think about it—were you surprised by the story Mika was telling herself as I shared my story? It's hard to imagine she'd rather have life-threatening cancer than a life-altering spinal injury.

After learning to listen to your own story, which lies in your subconscious, the next step is *listening to understand* the story others are telling themselves—searching to find and understand their story. Knowing how to listen differently to get to the story is fundamental to your success in implementing new processes, having a happy marriage, or negotiating a better price when buying a car.

Listening to your and their story creates a natural shift from telling to having a conversation; this shift is at the heart of effectively influencing others and negotiating.

GATHERING BEFORE TELLING

Since the inception of FMRI technology, the business world has been focused on the power of storytelling. Business is now all about telling a story that helps people see a new way and what the future could be. I agree with this notion and approach. However, I think the world has it wrong.

The most important thing is not the story you tell but the one you hear, the one you understand.

Understanding the story people are telling themselves ultimately informs the story you need to tell them.

The most important thing is not the story you tell but the one you hear, the one you understand.

EXERCISE

Describe a time when you had to change and how it made you feel.

_____

_____

_____

_____

CHAPTER SUMMARY

1. In 1991, functional magnetic resonance imaging (FMRI) was invented, enabling scientists to study the brain in real time. They discovered the emotional brain lights up when we buy or act. The conclusion is deciding to buy is emotional, not logical, as we once believed.

2. The cycle of how people act goes like this: an event happens, the subconscious tells a story about the event, that story creates a feeling, and the person acts based on that feeling.

3. The subconscious is in charge and always telling us a story.

4. The subconscious is more in charge of the conversation and is the enemy of listening.

5. Understanding the story we tell ourselves is why learning to listen to ourselves first is so important.

6. Helping people overcome the story they are telling themselves about change is a big part of sales and problem solving.

7. We tell ourselves stories and have biases based on our experience, upbringing, and other similar events. It is up to us to understand where our biases originate and the stories we tell ourselves so we can rise above the subconscious stories driving our beliefs and behaviors.

8. Storytelling has been the leading communication tool for the past decade. EQuipt believes the world has been getting it wrong. It's not the story you tell, but the one you get, the one you hear, the one you understand that is the most powerful form of communication.

9. Story Gathering is the precursor to storytelling. Understanding the story that people are telling themselves ultimately informs the story you need to tell them.

?

- Chapter 7 -

OVERCOMING BIAS

"People will forget what you said, people will forget what you did, but people will never forget how you made them feel."

— Maya Angelou

We can become more successful in our personal and work lives if we understand how people act or buy. We don't all need a degree in psychology, but understanding what lies below the surface with people, the approach psychologists take, will give you insight into how to get things done with buy-in, more effectively and more expeditiously.

The human brain has two parts: the conscious or logical brain, and the real superpower, the subconscious or emotional brain. Our subconscious brain is in charge, always telling us a story. That story affects how we feel and, therefore, how we act or don't act. Understanding the story we tell ourselves and finding out and understanding the story others are telling themselves are keys that open the door to greater emotional intelligence and listening differently. This positively influences every part of our life and helps us achieve.

WHAT STORY ARE THEY TELLING THEMSELVES ABOUT YOU?

Have you ever considered what story people are telling themselves about you? What is their first impression when someone meets you for the first time? What are their instant biases about you? Why do we fall in love, get married, and ten or twenty years later end up divorced? Well, in large part, the story our partner is telling themselves about us changes. Time and our behavior influence this story.

For example: "Before we had kids, we had a wonderful marriage; now, all she cares about are the kids and I'm always second." Or "Since he got a promotion, all he does is work all the time; he doesn't spend any time with me, but thankfully, I have the kids." We are back to death by 1,000 cuts. The person, the relationship, and the story aren't being attended to, listened to, or continually understood over years, and each small cut adds up to a gaping wound. The subconscious story becomes so great the relationship can't be repaired.

The story people are telling themselves about you is often based more on perception than reality.

Whether someone is meeting you for the first time or they've known you for decades, the story people are telling themselves about you is often based more on perception than reality. Unless both people are continually seeking what lies below the surface and understand more about each other, the story is one-dimensional. I learned this lesson when I was conducting diversity training for organizations while working at the EAP.

Most of the trainings were in short segments, anywhere from an hour to a few hours at the most. One thing I learned from the experience was the importance of making a big impact in a short period of time to quickly create shifts in people's thinking. I thought about what the audience members must be thinking when I was in front of the room teaching them. Let me paint the picture...I was twenty-eight, a white woman, from Hershey, and just by way of description, people often commented that I looked like Princess Diana because of my height and short blond hairstyle. I could only imagine that people were thinking: What the hell does Christine know about diversity? That was the story in my subconscious brain. So how could I quickly establish credibility and overcome this bias?

Whenever I went out to speak or conduct a workshop, I always started by telling my story to build credibility and help the audience understand where I was coming from. This time, I decided that rather than introducing myself by way of story, I would start by introducing the topic and talk about the primary and secondary dimensions of identity and diversity; primary being things we are born with, secondary being the things we choose. Then I would ask the audience, who had met me only a few minutes ago, to guess my primary and secondary dimensions of diversity. An interesting revelation unfolded over time. Regardless of where I went, who I was speaking to, the demographics, the type of company, etc., the answers were usually the same. People thought I was highly educated (true), married (true), from Connecticut or the South (not true), from an upper class family (not true), was Catholic (not true), had two children (not true), was not in the military (true), and so on. As you can see, they got about half right. This generated some very interesting discussion and also informed me how quickly people tell themselves a story about who you are, how inaccurate that story can be, and the importance of overcoming that bias.

EXERCISE

Write down three positive things people may be telling themselves about you when they meet you.

_____

_____

_____

Write down three negative things people may be telling themselves about you when they meet you.

_____

_____

_____

HOW YOU SHOW UP MAKES A DIFFERENCE

Have you ever considered what people think of you when you show up (present yourself), as a leader, a spouse, a parent, an employee, etc. What are people saying to themselves or to each other? Let me take you back to Atlanta; I shared in Chapter 2 that Lee Crump, the CIO of Rollins, commented on how the opening keynote of the CIO forum was so powerful. I promised we would get to this, and here we are.

To remind you, the goal of having me be part of the CIO events was to give the CIOs tools to connect on a more human level and bring those tools back to their organizations, and also to create more personal connections at the event with CIOs and the event company's partners.

The title of my keynote was, wait for it... "How You Show Up Makes a Difference." I believe the best method for learning, whether conducting a workshop or giving a keynote, is how surgeons are trained...tell them, show them, have them do, and then they can apply, or do it on their own. I started my keynote with the "tell them" portion. I set the foundation of the keynote, as I did with you, that employees want to be led by someone great, meaning someone who possesses the emotional skills. Then I had the audience watch the Michael Jr. Breaktime singing video so the audience could feel the difference when someone sings with purpose and passion, versus just sings competently. I then needed to show the audience "how" to show up differently live before their eyes.

Let me explain. I host a radio show called "Executive Leader's Radio" (ELR). It's a really special show created by Herb Cohen and run by Rachel Blumenthal, who is the executive producer and president. We have CEOs tell their story, specifically who they were between the ages of eight and fourteen, and how that relates to their success today.

One reason ELR recruited me was I was already helping people and organizations build this story. At EQuipt, we call this my purpose story (see Chapters 8 and 21).

Every week on the show, we interview four CEOs. It's a three-hour process from start to finish. What's so amazing is the CEOs stay the entire time, which is almost unheard of. The executives stay because they love the experience of hearing other CEOs' stories and looking at what they have in common in their respective backstories. The CEOs bond by the end of the show.

For my keynote address, "How You Show Up Makes a Difference," I decided to do a "mini ELR" interview live with a panel of three CIOs per city. During a typical panel discussion, CIOs are asked about their leadership style, beliefs, and best practices—mostly theoretical questions. Our spin was to have the CIOs share their backstory, specifically, to tell the audience about who they were between the ages of eight and fourteen and how that backstory affects their leadership today.

As yet another example of the story we tell ourselves and how it dictates how we relate to one another, when Lee Crump participated in the panel, I looked at his bio, which said he's a member of Mensa. As a dyslexic who struggled with academics early on, I admitted to Crump and the participants that I was a little intimidated by how smart he is.

Crump said, "Christine if it makes you feel any better, I only have an associate's degree. When I graduated from high school, I moved out on my own within two weeks, went into the service, and then got married. I never earned a college degree."

I heard the collective gasp from the audience at this revelation from a successful CIO who did not have a complete college education. I'm sure this wasn't the story people were telling themselves. Crump said when he became the CIO at Rollins, the first thing he did was to convince the CEO to remove the requirement that you must have a four-year college degree to work for the company. Crump's early life led him, decades later, to open the door to employees who may not have had the opportunity to earn a college degree and thus qualify to work at Rollins.

Understanding Crump's backstory helps us understand who he is today. It fast-tracks our connection to him. Who we were in our formative years influences who we are today, even if we don't think about it consciously. This was just one of Crump's stories we uncovered in a seven-minute interview.

The final portion of the keynote address was the "do" portion. I asked the audience to turn to the person to their right and ask them some of the questions I had asked Crump about his backstory. I had them ask about things like: How young was this person when they started earning money? What did their mom and dad do for a living? How many siblings did they have? What activities were they involved in? What activities did they do on teams or with family?

What happened next always thrilled me. An immediate eruption of laughter and talk filled the large banquet halls. You could feel the passion and see people mirroring each other as they talked. Meaningful connections were being made by way of hearing each other's story.

This exercise came early in the day, and ultimately, shaped how people presented themselves, spoke to one another, and connected throughout the entire event. In the end, they were ready to take this tool back to their organizations and apply what they learned.

Have you considered all the things you don't know about the people you are meeting for the first time or what you have in common? What don't you know about the people you have known or worked with for twenty years? We tend to think there's nothing new to learn when we've known someone for that long. In reality, most of who they are, their story, is going on below the surface, and we never think to ask ourselves or others to tell us their story.

EXERCISE

Answer these questions to understand who you were between the ages of eight and fourteen.

How many siblings do you have?

_____

What did your mom do for a living?

_____

What did your dad do for a living?

_____

What does the number of siblings you had and what your parents did for a living have to do with why you do what you do today?

_____

_____

_____

MEETING YOU IN THE MIDDLE OF YOUR MOVIE

Why is it so important to understand someone's backstory when you meet them? Does their backstory really matter? I often say our lives are like a movie. What happens when you miss the beginning of a movie and start watching twenty minutes in? Usually, people feel confused. "What did I miss? Who is that? How did it start? I'm not sure what's going on."

Now let's go to someone meeting us. Why would someone meeting us be any different? We expect people to trust us because we tell them we are trustworthy or have good intentions, experience, or credentials. They really don't know who we are, and we often just tell them what we do or what we want them to do. Therefore, they make up their own story about who we are, much like when I was doing diversity training. The bias is formed without considering the process happening below the surface. The story people tell themselves about us either helps or hinders our ability to influence and lead them. Unfortunately, it's usually the latter since we represent a change, and we already looked at how people feel about change.

SHAPING THE STORY

Did you know you can shape the story people tell themselves about you? When you meet them, if you tell them who you are first, take them back to the beginning, the origin of who you are, you will get a running start at helping them figure out who you are now and why they can believe in you.

In the spring of 2019, I met an incredible woman and leader named Milena. She had worked for some pretty big-name brands and was about to start a new position at a well-known apparel company based in Florida. Milena lives in Northern New Jersey and was going to be leading a team of about thirty-five people, mostly located in Florida. This was at the beginning of the pandemic when the entire world was working virtually so Milena would not be working in person with her new team anytime soon.

Milena and I met when I was moderating a virtual summit where thought leaders from around the world were sharing their perspectives on how the pandemic would change the future of business. Milena had just received the offer and was to start in about a month. She asked if I would be willing to help her build her story so she could introduce herself to the team in a personal way, as she had seen me do with the thought leaders.

Some leaders are reluctant to talk about themselves; they'd rather keep the focus on their employees. While I certainly understand this, it does miss the point a little. To focus on others, it helps to lift the veil and show them who you are first. Then they feel safer. Remember the mirror neurons? Milena understood and was undaunted by the idea of being vulnerable.

I helped build Milena's story, and I was delighted when she called to tell me how sharing her story with her team went. Milena said she opened her first team meeting by going back to her beginning and even used personal pictures to help tell her story. She took her team on the path of where she began, the struggles she faced, and how she got to where she is leading them today. Milena said after the meeting, the company president, who had been on the team call, commented on how effective sharing her story was. In the end, Milena was grateful that telling her story ultimately helped her team get to know who she was quickly and showed them why she was there and why she does what she does.

Milena's team quickly mirrored her frankness and shared more about themselves, helping her understand not just what they do, but who they are. Milena got to know her team and bonded with them more quickly, enabling them all to get things done together more effectively—all without ever being in the same room with them.

Have you ever noticed that you are more inclined to share a story about yourself when someone tells you a story about themselves? When they do, are you ready to listen differently?

EXERCISE

Think of a time when you shared a story about yourself and it allowed you to bond with someone or a team you were working with.

_____

_____

_____

CHAPTER SUMMARY

1. We are all biased, and people are always telling themselves a story.

2. Impressions based on our biases are formed as soon as we meet someone. The story people tell themselves about us enhances or diminishes our ability to influence and lead them.

3. The story people tell themselves about us is often based more on perception than reality.

4. People meet us in the middle of our life's movie. People are confused, disoriented, and not sure if they should trust us without knowing the beginning of our life story.

5. You can shape the story people tell themselves by lifting your veil and telling your story.

6. When you tell your story, others are more likely to mirror you and share more about themselves. This helps create a bond, builds trust, and promotes understanding on a deeper level.

7. We tend to think there's nothing new to learn when we've known somebody for a long time. In reality, most of us have a lot going on below the surface, and most never think to ask about the big chunk of ice floating below the surface. To foster relationships, we must continually seek to understand.

?

- Chapter 8 -

KNOWING YOUR PURPOSE

"The meaning of life is to find your gift.
The purpose of life is to give it."

— *Pablo Picasso*

O vercoming biases and the stories people tell themselves about you is part of the journey to Transformational Listening. When we take the time to listen and understand, or even hypothesize about what story people are telling themselves, we start breaking down barriers and connecting. We are learning to listen to what isn't said and think about the other person first.

Our life is like a movie, and people are essentially meeting us in the middle of that movie. We expect them to trust us, to believe we have good intentions and have their best interests at heart. That's a lot to ask when we aren't showing people the first twenty minutes of our movie. If we take people back to the beginning, we help them better understand how we became who we are; we facilitate connection and trust.

One principle of psychology is that the best predictor of future behavior is past behavior. Others are more comfortable with what you will do now and in the future when they've seen what you've done or believed previously. Building trust, overcoming biases, and the stories others tell themselves about you may seem like it could take years, but you can actually move the needle in mere minutes. It's a matter of sharing who you are, your purpose, and why you do what you do, or as we say at EQuipt, your "My Purpose Story."

When you lift your veil and tell your story, you help others feel like it's okay to open up and tell you theirs, and the listening floodgates are opened.

The "My Purpose Story" is the story of how young you were when you discovered your purpose, and the path you traveled to fulfill that purpose. This story helps people understand who you really are and more deeply connect with you.

When you lift your veil and tell your story, you help others feel like it's okay to open up and tell you theirs, and the listening floodgates are opened.

PEOPLE CARE HOW YOU BECAME GREAT, NOT HOW GREAT YOU ARE

Have you ever considered what your real purpose is? Have you thought about why you do what you do and where that purpose comes from?

I have some good news and some slightly bad news here. The good news is it's really pretty easy to share your *my purpose story*, and you reap the benefits quickly. The slightly bad news is it's a little harder to go back to when you found your purpose and really try to understand how you found it so you can build this story.

Let's first start with the good news—an example of how telling your *my purpose story* creates a quick connection with the listener. My team and I have been working with a company called Brewer Science, which is a really special company. It is relatively small compared to its competitors, yet it is the world leader in materials for microelectronics. The company culture is focused on caring for their people, which contributes greatly to their incredible success. The chief resource officer (CRO), Dan Brewer, saw the value of further bolstering the human resources team's ability to listen and create a common approach of empathy and insight. Dan and the human resources team have a growth mindset, so the entire human resources team went through the Listening Path workshop to improve their listening ability.

Following the workshop, we conducted our 360-feedback process in which we listen to a cross-section of people to gain greater insight into how the human resources team can best serve the organization at large. Our approach includes interviewing the company's ten most senior leaders.

At Brewer Science, each interview was conducted virtually and took about an hour. I was scheduled to meet with the chief science officer, whom I'll call Brenda. She had been with Brewer for close to twenty-five years. She was not native to the United States, though she had lived here since her twenties when she came to the US to earn her doctorate. I learned Brenda had two master's degrees in engineering and was just shy of completing her doctorate in chemical engineering. Needless to say, I knew this woman was very smart before I met her.

When we started the call, Brenda greeted me with a smile and a warmth that beamed through my computer screen. This was not at all what I was expecting from a left-brained, science type with multiple degrees in engineering—yet another story I had told myself that wasn't accurate. Oh, how quickly our biases form misperceptions.

At the start of our meeting, I took a moment to describe what we would be doing over the course of the hour, and then, as I always do, I told her my purpose story (in less than three minutes), leading off with, "If I had one word to describe why I do what I do, it would be *understanding*," and so on.

When I finished my story, I turned to Brenda and said, "Now, please tell me more about you."

As we continued to talk, Brenda shared a very personal story of how, while she was in her doctoral program, one of her professors sexually harassed her. She was alone and felt vulnerable because her husband was in another state, so she decided to leave the program. She told me more, mentioning that as hard as leaving was, she had already gotten everything she needed out of the program, including learning how to think to solve problems.

Brenda said, "I got everything I needed. I just didn't get the degree or title." I was impressed by her humility and strength. We had talked for about ten minutes, and when she finished her story, she smiled and looked at me through the screen. She said, "Christine, you are very good at what you do. I've never told anybody here that story."

I must admit I was tempted to take credit for being so magnificent, but I knew better; it wasn't me at all. Instead, I fessed up and, leaning into my screen, said, "Well, I'm going to tell you a little secret. I told you my story, so your subconscious would tell you it was okay for you to tell me yours." She smiled at me and said, "Maybe I should tell my team that story sometime."

In addition to the great gift of knowing this wonderful woman more deeply, two lessons came to mind about starting relationships by telling your purpose story.

First, when you share your purpose story, people will mirror your actions and tell you more about who they are. If you really listen, you will learn more in ten minutes than some people learn about others in twenty years.

Second, in my experience, people really don't care about how great we are, how many degrees we have, or what we've accomplished—what they really care about are the struggles we went through to become great.

YOUR ONE-WORD PURPOSE

How do you take your whole purpose and simplify it, narrowing it down to one single word? I know you are wondering about this because so many of our clients ask. Let's go back to that slightly bad news about the heavier task of uncovering your purpose and simplify the process. Believe it or not, you'll be able to pare your purpose down to one word pretty quickly. No matter what we do, what title or position we have, our purpose tends to come to us early in life, and that purpose endures regardless of the title or position we hold at any point.

As I've mentioned before, our clients are our best teachers. Sometimes I wonder if we learn more from them than they learn from us. One of our long-term clients is Tozour Energy Systems, a leader in the heating, ventilation, and air conditioning (HVAC) industry.

Kevin Duffy, the president, and Frank Rhea, the executive vice president, are two leaders who know the power of investing in their people. Not only have they provided coaching for their leaders and employees over the years, but they have also invested in training almost everyone in the company on the Listening Path.

About twelve years ago, my team and I were working with young professionals in the service part of the business. Frank had the vision and foresight to structure the organization in such a way that the customer service reps (CSRs) became the pipeline for the future sales, operations, and leadership positions. Frank also understood that more women were needed in the HVAC industry and largely looked for young women professionals he could hire as CSRs to develop and learn the business from the ground up.

Our early work with Frank's team included individual coaching. One day, as we were conducting a coaching assessment, I met separately with four of the CSRs on Frank's team. They were all women in their early twenties to early thirties. During one conversation, I thought, *Why are these young professionals so excited to be working for Tozour in the HVAC industry, climbing up on rooftops, talking to facility managers and technicians?* I had been up on those rooftops, and it wasn't glamourous at all.

My initial thought was, *Well, of course, Tozour is a great company and very well regarded and they offer a lot of opportunity for growth.* Instead of assuming, I decided to ask one of the CSRs this question: Why are you excited to be in the HVAC business?

The answer was unexpected.

The CSR said, "I like helping people."

I was a bit perplexed since I wasn't sure what HVAC had to do with helping people. Fortunately, my curiosity got the better of me, so I asked her to tell me more. She said, "I get to help solve problems for our customers, deal with their emergencies, make their employees and tenants more comfortable in their buildings, and make sure they get the best products at the best price. We are helping our customers deal with crises throughout the day. I love the feeling of being able to help."

I was so intrigued by her answer that I decided to ask the other three CSRs, and, to my amazement, I got almost the exact same answer from each. They all said they liked helping people. This is where we got the idea for beginning to tell your purpose in one word. The one word all four CSRs said was "helping."

Now that you see it's not as hard as you might've thought, have you considered what your one word might be? I know it can be challenging to pick only one word, but my experience is fewer options make it easier to choose. Think about a time you went to buy something—it's easier to choose when there are only two choices instead of fifty. I remind people that the word you start with is not necessarily the word you'll end up with, but most of the time, it's pretty close. Here are some of the one-word purposes from my team:

Voice	More	Connection
Reflection	Needs	Farming
Explore	Others	Seen
Curiosity	Serve	

I'll use my team member Dean as an example of how one word defines our purpose. Dean's word is "explore." Dean started backpacking the Appalachian Trail with his best friend when he was thirteen. Learning to follow the clues from nature was an inspiration for him in how he views himself and in solving problems. Dean spent a large part of his career solving complex problems in large technology organizations, exploring how to create the best solutions.

Another example is with my team member Matt. Matt grew up with a single mom and three sisters. At age sixteen, he started his own mobile detailing business, and by age seventeen, he was earning seven thousand dollars a month, which he used to help support his mom and family. Matt saw the impact he had on his family and now wants to have an impact on others in his life and career.

EXERCISE

If you had only one word to describe why you do what you do, what would that word be?

YOUR ELEVATOR STORY

How many times have you gone to a networking event, a customer meeting, an internal meeting, or even a dinner party where they have you go around the table and introduce yourself? What usually happens? Everyone introduces themselves by saying their name, who they work for, what they do, and how long they've been there.

In my experience, this is a mind-numbing exercise, and in general, adds very little and creates very little interest or conversation. How can we shift the paradigm? Corporate America is all about having a "brand." Do you have an executive presence, and how do you differentiate yourself? One of the necessary evils of sharing your brand is the typical elevator pitch—I prefer to call it your elevator story.

The paradigm shift is to think about your elevator story this way: You can tell me both why you do what you do and a little about who you are in one word, one or two sentences, and/or in a two-to-three-minute story, which is far more memorable and interesting than your name and title.

Back to Tozour and Frank. After we taught Frank's team how to create their one word and elevator stories, Frank had his team introduce themselves that way at their next client meeting.

The customer told Frank they had never had such a great initial meeting and felt they really got to know the team they would be working with, which built a lot of confidence. Tozour ultimately won the customer and, while it wasn't the only factor, Frank said it was clear that the way they introduced themselves was an important factor in getting the deal.

Listening to our customers, understanding how they apply what we teach them, and the difference it made in their business has made us better and smarter. What is your purpose story? Is it balanced or more focused on your career or personal life? What is the one word to describe your purpose?

EXERCISE

Write down your purpose in a few sentences, starting with your one word.

_____

_____

_____

_____

CHAPTER SUMMARY

1. The best predictor of future behavior is past behavior; this is why storytelling is such a powerful communication tool.

2. Stories share what has already been done.

3. People do not care how great you are; they care about what you went through to become great.

4. Building trust may seem like it could take years, but you can move the needle in mere minutes. All it takes is sharing the story of who you are, your purpose, and why you do what you do.

5. We all have a passion and a purpose. Tapping into that purpose starts with picking one word that describes why you do what you do.

6. Our purpose tends to come to us early in life, our beginning, no matter what we do or what title or position we have. Our purpose endures regardless of the title or position we hold at any point.

7. When you lift your veil and share your purpose, you help others feel okay about sharing theirs and the listening floodgates open.

8. We start breaking down barriers and connect when we take the time to listen and understand, or even hypothesize about which story people may be telling themselves.

9. People will mirror your behavior and tell you more about who they are after you share your purpose story. If you really listen, you will learn more in ten minutes than some people learn about someone in twenty years.

?

SECTION TWO

LISTENING DIFFERENTLY

*"The improvement of understanding is for two ends:
first, our own increase of knowledge; secondly, to
enable us to deliver that knowledge to others."*

— John Locke

?

- Chapter 9 -

STORY GATHERING VERSUS ATTENTIVE LISTENING

"The first duty of love is to listen."

— *Paul Tillich*

Part of transforming how you listen is presenting yourself in a way that helps people understand who you are and overcome the story they may be telling themselves about you in their subconscious. We all have a purpose that typically shows up very early in life. When we tap into this purpose and can share it in one word, one sentence, or one story, it helps others see it's okay to share their story. Then, the magic of listening differently begins.

Now that we understand why listening is so critical, it's time to learn how to listen differently. Before we go forward, let's take a quick step back.

SUMMARIZING WHERE WE'VE BEEN

Let's take a moment to review what we've covered so far. Our subconscious is in charge. It is the brain's superpower, where our emotions and stories lie. Everyone has a story. Everyone tells themselves a story. We all have unconscious biases and fear of the unknown. These stories inform what we believe and don't believe, how we act or don't act.

I believe most people are not taught to understand what they are feeling, why they are feeling what they're feeling, or which stories they are telling themselves. Many of us are on autopilot. It is my experience that this is also true not only with self-awareness, but also our awareness and understanding of others. I don't mean for that to sound condescending or critical. Most of us are simply not taught how to be aware of emotions and the stories in the subconscious, let alone taught the language to describe what's going on to ourselves or others.

We do not devote enough education or resources to the cause. We get zero years of education on listening, and only 2 percent of people have had any type of listening training. The emotional skills, and especially the skill of listening, have historically been assumed—one is born with them, developed them early, or doesn't have them. Until the invention of FMRI technology, we weren't even sure people could develop emotional skills. You were stuck with what you had or didn't have. We now know the brain is flexible, and new pathways can be formed through repetition. With the right help and tools, we can build these skills.

Listening to ourselves and others is how we start to build new pathways and overcome the stories we tell ourselves and the stories others tell about us. We reshape how we communicate and interact with each other. We break down walls through understanding. This understanding earns us the right to help others solve problems. Listening helps us discover the story of our passion and purpose and tap into our one word. This changes how we present ourselves and enables us to influence people and get them to opt in and follow. Listening enables us to sing better than competently, in a much more inspirational way.

The business world has been focused on storytelling as the main communication vehicle of change and influence since neuroscience proved in 1994 that we buy emotionally. I fervently believe the world has been getting it all wrong. The most powerful communication and influence vehicle is not storytelling, not what we say, or what we tell. The most powerful vehicle of communication is to transform how we listen and the stories we gather.

EXERCISE

Write down the three things that have made the biggest impression on you thus far in the book.

_____

_____

_____

_____

HEARING, THE SENSE THAT GETS US VERY LITTLE

How do we learn to gather a story? How do we understand the story others are telling themselves and learn to be more empathetic? How do we learn to hear what is not said and see what we can't see with our eyes? The answer is to learn how to listen differently, in a transformational way.

Transformational Listening is a dialogue between the teller and the listener. The listener and the teller are in an exchange, and they connect and bond along the path—changing the way conversations happen. Just like there are different levels of running, as my friend Deb taught me, there are different levels of listening. Deb broke down the skill and showed me how to take my running and quickness to the next level. I'll do the same for you, so let's start at the most basic level of listening—hearing.

According to Webster's Dictionary, hearing is defined as "the process, function, or power of perceiving sound specifically." I'm sure that hearing as a sense—what the ear actually takes in—is not a revelation to you. This, however, may be more of a revelation. According to Credit Dorney Research, statistically, "We only retain 17 to 25 percent of what we hear." In what other project or process would 17 to 25 percent be seen as a success?

I equate relying on the sense of hearing to going out 300 miles in the middle of the ocean to fish with a rowboat and one ore.

Most of us are relying on our sense of hearing to listen, get the story, and understand what is going on with the teller. Metaphorically, I equate relying on the sense of hearing to going out 300 miles in the middle of the ocean to fish with a rowboat and one ore. You're simply not properly equipped to catch any fish, let alone return safely. Our sense of hearing does not equip us with what we need to navigate the deep waters and what is going on below the surface.

How many times have you said to your partner or child, "Are you listening?" They say yes and repeat exactly what you just said. Sure, they heard the words, but you feel frustrated or upset and woefully unsatisfied because, while they heard your words, they didn't understand what you meant and no action followed. Hearing has very little to do with being understood and is the most rudimental level of listening.

BEING ATTENTIVE IS ONLY PART OF IT

How do we take listening to the next level? How do we go from simply hearing the words to something better? Historically, listening effectively or actively has been synonymous with "attentive listening." Attentive listening, by definition, means to attend or pay attention to the teller and what the teller is saying. It is what most listening training is focused on. Spoiler alert—while I still believe being attentive is part of good listening, I do not believe it is as effective as the world has come to believe. A big part of the problem is that attentive listening tells you what behaviors to do, but not how to do them. Let me slow down here—bear with me—the slow down will help you in the end to get where we are going faster.

I ask clients, "What does it look like when someone is listening effectively or attentively?" I'll ask you the same thing: What do you think attentive or effective listening looks like?

EXERCISE

Take a moment to write three things you are doing when you are listening attentively.

_____

_____

_____

_____

Your answers, like our clients' answers, are probably pretty much the same and for good reason. This is all the world has taught us about what it means to be an attentive listener. Here is what the world considers the best practices in listening:

- Giving the person thoughtful attention
- Being curious
- Empathizing
- Listening with your eyes
- Repeating what you hear

Let's take a short pause and think about the term "listening effectively." Effective means producing a desired or intended result. If your desire is to have a teller feel like you are attentive to them, then you may achieve success. I don't believe that is nearly enough. While attentive listening can help make you a more competent listener, like being a competent singer, you still don't stand out in the crowd. There are different skill levels in listening. We can all sing. Some of us can sing well or competently, but very few can sing in an inspiring way. To me, there is nothing inspiring about the concept of listening effectively or attentively. It's a step in the right direction, and it's better than what most of us do, but I believe it still under-delivers. We are basically teaching people to underdeliver.

Let's look at the list of things we are doing when we are being competent or attentive listeners. Giving thoughtful attention—what does that mean? Usually, the answer we get is about making eye contact with the person. I'll show them I am paying attention by looking them in the eyes. Talk about a low bar! I'll look at you to prove that I'm listening. The other problem is that the value of making eye contact is culturally specific.

I remember talking about the importance of eye contact some twenty years ago while conducting a communication workshop while working at the EAP. I was moved by a gentleman who said he was born and raised in a country where making eye contact was disrespectful. After seventeen years living in the United States, he said he still had to force himself to make eye contact with people. We tend to think that what we want is what we should give to other people, and we often get it wrong by making this kind of assumption.

Up next—being curious. What does it mean to be curious? The answer that we most often get about curiosity is that it means you are asking good questions. That is certainly part of curiosity, but the actual definition of curiosity is the strong desire to know or learn more. Questions can be a vehicle to express the desire to know more, but in my experience, they can also be a real interference in the listening process (more on this in Chapter 11).

Now let's look at being empathetic. Sure, just be more empathetic! If only it was that easy. If most people knew how to be more empathetic, we wouldn't have a drought of emotional acuity. The idea that we simply tell someone to be more empathetic and they will just be able to do it is particularly frustrating to me. We are blaming the listener when it's not their fault. We are not socialized to be curious about emotions and feelings, whether they are our feelings or the feelings of others.

We are not socialized to be curious about emotions and feelings, whether they are our feelings or the feelings of others.

For many of us, emotions, particularly bad ones, make us uncomfortable and for good reason. I don't want you to feel bad. I don't know what to do about it when you tell me how bad you feel. I don't know how to make it better, and all of this makes me feel bad too.

Listening with your eyes. What does that mean? Communication studies have been done for decades, and it has been largely understood that most communication is nonverbal rather than verbal. While statistics may vary a bit, including intonation, estimates run as high as 93 percent of communication being nonverbal. Listening with your eyes means paying attention to the non-verbal cues, watching the person's body language, and hearing how something is said.

Last, but not least, let's look at repeating or reflecting what the person has said. This, for sure, is a very good practice when it comes to listening. However, most of us hear only a small portion of what is actually said. Even more of us are not socialized to hear, address, or repeat emotions. The emotions are often not heard at all or ignored. Repeating what one hears can turn into an exercise in parroting, where the words are heard, but the meaning is lost. Like when you ask your kid to clean up their room, but they don't. You ask again and they say, "I heard you." They heard the words, but not the message. Despite the good intentions of repeating what one hears, it can still leave the teller feeling unheard or misunderstood.

While all these behaviors seem like they help us listen, our problem is not really solved by learning to be an attentive listener. It is simply not enough. Attending to the listener is important, but not as important as how to listen in a way that creates a bond and uncovers the real insight. We need to learn more about how to listen differently.

WHAT VERSUS HOW

Do you see how attentive listening tells people what to do to listen better, but not how to do it? Attentive listening can still be a rather passive and one-way endeavor. After introducing the topic of attentive listening in our workshops and asking the participants what attentive listening looks like, we go through the list as I did with you just now. Then I often joke by saying, "Okay, training over. You're all set. Now go out and listen. You know what to do; just go do it." Everyone chuckles because they realize that knowing what attentive listening is has little to do with being able to listen differently.

Even for the 2 percent of people who have had listening training, that training was focused on the list of behaviors we outlined above, and they, while slightly better listeners than they were before the training, admitted they still struggled.

One of my coaches and *listening gurus*, Sue, told a story of how she went through a two-day attentive listening course when she earned her executive coaching certification. It was part of the curriculum. She was already a good listener but, by her own admission, still often missed the mark. Sue told me they spent a lot of time in the course asking the right questions.

After going through only a half-day of a Listening Path workshop, Sue was amazed by how her listening transformed. She learned our framework and the tools, which she could easily use, made sense. This was a big reason for her wanting to work with EQuipt. What she learned in her coaching course was all about asking questions, a big part of how attentive listening is taught. She said, "I was so busy thinking about the questions to ask that I was in my brain and missing the message and failing as a listener." With the Listening Path, you don't have to think about the questions at all. How often are you stuck in your brain, thinking about what to ask and missing the message?

THE NEW PARADIGM: STORY GATHERING

Why are we getting it so wrong even when we are making an effort? Attentive listening misses the mark—the world has been getting it wrong. We can do better; we have to do better. To transform the way we listen and create a two-way, meaningful conversation that leads to connection, problems getting solved,

To transform the way we listen and create a two-way, meaningful conversation that leads to connection, problems getting solved, and things getting done, we need to move to a new method, a whole different level of listening.

and things getting done, we need to move to a new method, a whole different level of listening. This is done by shifting from just attending to the teller to gathering their story, both the facts and feelings. That is, to go beyond hearing what is said to also hearing what is not said and creating an exchange, a shared experience, discovering something, finding the hidden gem in the conversation, and uncovering the insight or the meaning.

Sometimes the teller already knows the insight of their story; sometimes, the listener is the one who discovers the insight for the teller. Either way, it's a joint adventure of discovery, where both the listener and the teller are walking together on the same path, on a journey of understanding. The new paradigm is called Story Gathering.

Imagine you listen to your spouse in a transformational way where you hear what they're not saying and help them understand something new about themselves? How would that change your relationship? How about with your customers—imagine what it would feel like if you helped them realize something they didn't see or know about a problem they were dealing with. What are the chances they would trust you enough to buy your service or product? When you gather the full story and uncover the insight, you earn the right to help them solve problems.

It's funny; over the years many of my clients have said, "Christine, for some reason I don't mind it when you tell me something about myself I don't want to hear, and I'm not sure why that is." Sometimes, I let them in on the secret. It's because I have taken the time to listen in a way that I get their full story. They feel deeply understood, seen, appreciated, and cared for. When I am Story Gathering, people know I care, and I genuinely do. I am able to help them hear something that may be uncomfortable because I slowed down to gather their story first. That earned me the right to tell them something they may not want to hear, and ultimately, helps them personally, in their career.

Are you ready to slow down to listen differently and learn how to story gather? It's worthwhile, but not always easy.

EXERCISE

Share an experience where you story gathered. How did that shift the conversation?

_____

_____

_____

_____

CHAPTER SUMMARY

1. Hearing and listening are different. Statistically, we retain only 17 to 25 percent of what we hear.

2. Hearing has very little to do with being understood and is the most basic level of listening.

3. When we rely on our sense of hearing to listen, get the story, and understand, metaphorically, it's like going out 300 miles in the middle of the ocean to fish with a rowboat and one ore.

4. Attentive listening is the old paradigm for listening. Attentive listening is essentially learning how to "attend" to the listener.

5. Attentive listening tells someone what to do—be present, empathize, reflect—but not how to do it.

6. The new paradigm for listening is Story Gathering, which is a joint adventure of discovery where both the listener and the teller walk together on the same path, on a journey of understanding. When you gather the full story and uncover the insight, you earn the right to help solve problems.

?

Chapter 10

LISTENING IS SO HARD

"There is a difference between listening and
waiting for your turn to speak."

— *Simon Sinek*

The difference between what has historically, and I believe incorrectly, been the gold standard of listening effectively, attentive listening, and what we at EQuipt call Story Gathering is vast. Story Gathering is the process of Transformational Listening that uncovers what is and what is not said.

The first level of listening is hearing, a rudimentary sense that allows us to perceive words. The next level is attentive listening where the listener focuses on the behaviors that show the teller they are attending to them as a person and to their words when they are listening.

Attentive listing involves things like making eye contact, showing empathy, being curious, asking the right questions, listening with your eyes, and repeating what you heard. While attending to the listener differently is a step in the right direction, the approach has a couple of problems.

First, attentive listening tells you what to do but not how to do it. The attentive listener isn't armed with the tools they need to change how they listen. Second, only attending often leaves the teller feeling very unsatisfied about what the listener actually heard and understood. Attentive listening doesn't necessarily lead to insight and is a more passive approach to listening. Attentive listening is like this: As your listener, I will attend to you while you talk, make sure you know I am paying attention, and be present.

In contrast, Story Gathering is a very active process and a shared journey between the listener and the teller, where together they follow the same path to understanding and insight.

I realize you are probably thinking, *How do I become a story gatherer and transform how I listen? Christine, you haven't told me how to do it yet? When the hell are you going to tell me?* Not to worry; I have been dropping little breadcrumbs along the way into your subconscious so soon the pieces of the puzzle will start to come together.

I wish I could tell you that making something simple is easy to do. When we're learning something new and intangible, confusion and uncertainty are part of the journey. Please stay with me; I promise I will make it worth your while.

Have you ever wondered why listening is so hard? I'm about to help you better understand why you are failing and what's interfering with your success. This will help you pivot more quickly in the end. Slowing down to speed up again. Ironically, confusion and uncertainty will occur as you're gathering a story as well. Sticking with it and following the path will be key to your success. See, listening is really hard. As I have said, the subconscious is a superpower, the one in charge, the one in control. When we're listening, our subconscious is firing on all cylinders and telling us to do everything—except listen, that is.

> **When we're listening, our subconscious is firing on all cylinders and telling us to do everything—except listen, that is.**

LISTENING INHIBITORS

As I told you early in this book, not being a good listener is not your fault. And even if you're already a good listener but want to be better and are struggling to get to that next level, that isn't your fault either. Do you know why? Let's talk a little bit more about the subconscious and what is happening when we try to listen. What follows is a list of what we call listening inhibitors. These are things that are happening in our subconscious when we try to listen that we are unaware of.

EXERCISE

Check the listening inhibiters you are guilty of. Check all that apply to you.

Inhibitors
to listening

Needing to be right

Mind reading

Rehearsing

Filtering

Judging

Being the expert

With only ears

Advising/problem solving

Sparring

Placating

Distracted by technology

Uncomfortable with silence

Talking too much

How many did you check? Write down the three listening inhibitors you are most guilty of.

_____

_____

_____

_____

Not to worry; you're not alone. When we ask our clients what they're guilty of, most people say, "I'm guilty of all of them." Even if you are a good or great listener, it's easy to fall prey to these inhibitors. The ones consistently at the top of the list are rehearsing, mind reading, and advising/problem-solving. We'll look at talking too much and being distracted by technology in a moment.

Let's start with rehearsing, a very common listening inhibitor. When someone is talking, our subconscious is telling us a story. Commonly, that story is, "What am I going to say when they are done talking? How am I going to respond? I better figure out what I am going to say, or I'm going to look pretty stupid." We're so busy thinking about and rehearsing in our head how we are going to respond that we totally miss what the teller just said.

Now, let's look at mind reading. Unfortunately, for some reason, people expect they should be able to read another person's thoughts. They think it's somehow more meaningful if they are able to anticipate or know what someone is going to say rather than give them the space just to tell their story.

I'll never forget when we were working with a leadership team a few years back. As we were going through the listening inhibitors and asking which ones they were guilty of, we got to mind reading. One of the leaders raised his hand and said, "I don't mind read, but I can tell when other people do." The room erupted in laughter. Such is the absurdity of our subconscious. Trying to read someone's mind rather than just listening is like guessing the next turn rather than letting your GPS guide you. Why not take the easier way?

SOLVING THE PROBLEM HAS THE OPPOSITE EFFECT

Next up is problem solving and/or advising. This listening inhibitor is, notably, the most reported. Do you remember how I said experience is the enemy of listening? The more experience and knowledge we have, the more likely we are to rush to solve the problem.

Here's what's so fascinating about problem-solving: most people who want to solve the problem are trying to be helpful. I often tease and joke with our workshop participants or audiences. "How dare you! You're such an asshole for not wanting to see me struggle and telling me how to solve my problem so it actually gets fixed." Problem solving falls under the category of no good deed goes unpunished. The intention of the problem solver, whether a leader, spouse, parent, or salesperson, is usually to be helpful. Unfortunately, the results are that the teller is frustrated and thinks, *I just wanted you to listen.*

Remember, no one likes to be told what to do. When was the

last time you started to solve a problem for someone before you listened to understand? Did you see the nail in the forehead and want to take it out?

EXERCISE

Reflect upon and write down what it might have cost you the last time your brain went into problem solving mode rather than listening.

_____

_____

_____

_____

TALKING KILLS RESULTS

Do you think people talk too much? Do you ever feel frustrated in meetings or conversations because someone just won't stop talking or tends to dominate by speaking all the time? Quite honestly, I'm probably not the best person to judge how the general population is feeling on the subject of people talking too much. As someone in the business of listening, I am acutely aware of how much time people spend talking instead of listening, whether I'm in the conversation or observing it. The CIA has a famous quote, "Silence sucks the truth out." Go figure—shutting up gets so much more of what we need to know than talking. Yet too many of us spend most of our time talking and telling.

A few years ago, I was meeting with a senior vice president of sales. The day before, my team and I conducted a Listening Path workshop for the sales and customer service teams and all the executives participated. As I was walking to the VP's office, many people greeted me—smiling, giving me a high-five, and thanking me for the day before and the great experience it was. Shortly after I sat down in the VP's office, a new sales rep who had just started that day knocked on the door, specifically to introduce himself. I saw him watching my interactions with people on my way to the VP's office. He was astute in noticing I might have influence and it would be smart to introduce himself to me.

At that point, I was intrigued by his curiosity. The well-dressed, extroverted sales representative in his early thirties opened the door and put out his hand. "Hi, I'm Jason." He spent about five minutes telling me about himself, his resume, and how excited he was to be working at the company. I just listened, as did his new boss. When he was finished, Jason said, "Well, I just wanted to introduce myself. I'll let you get back to your meeting."

Jason left and closed the door. The VP turned and looked at me, saying, "I'm so excited we hired him. He's going to be great with the customers." I asked him to tell me more, and he went on to talk about how good Jason was in front of people.

I had a totally different feeling. What I observed was that Jason was good at talking and catching someone's attention. My worry was he was not a good listener and would struggle with customers after the initial introductions. When I shared my thoughts with the VP, he said, "How can you know that in such a short interaction?" He challenged my perspective pretty hard. I said, "Jason spent the entire time talking about himself and, while he thought I may have influence, he didn't stop to listen or ask about me. I'm not invested in Jason knowing me, but I felt it was all about Jason because he spent so much time talking. I believe your customers are going to feel this too." Sales happen when you listen and discover something—talking too much inhibits this.

There's a longer story here that involves a bet between the VP and me as to whether Jason would struggle because he talked too much. Three months later, the VP graciously acknowledged that what I saw in the initial meeting was exactly the struggle Jason was having with customers, and the VP paid up. Talking kills results. Have you ever considered how much time you spend talking instead of listening?

EXERCISE

How do you feel when someone talks twice as much as they listen?

_____

_____

_____

_____

On a scale of 1 to 100 percent, on average, how much time do you spend listening instead of talking? Rate the percentage in the three different scenarios over the past week:

An individual meeting

_____

A group or team meeting

_____

A conversation with a friend

_____

LISTENING IN THE DIGITAL AGE

Have you ever considered the negative effect digital technology (computers, phones, social media, etc.) is having on your personal and business relationships? How much is technology interfering with or eroding your ability to listen? As a Gen Xer, I think people like me who didn't grow up with digital technology see the younger generations as the ones whose communication, people connection, and listening skills are lacking due to growing up with technology. Let me challenge that notion for you: it's not just the younger generations; it's us too.

According to a study by Gearbrand, "In 2020, US adults spend seven hours and fifteen minutes a day on smart phones, desktops, and other devices watching content and engaging with online apps. This is expected to surpass eight hours a day by the year 2022. That's more than the average adult spends sleeping."

Digital technology has provided access to things we could never have imagined, and it would certainly be difficult to go back to life without it. This same technology has also been a connector and made the world a smaller place. There is no better example of this than in 2020 during the pandemic lockdown. Think about the number of Zoom or Microsoft Teams calls we had to keep our businesses running. Or how we had Thanksgiving dinner, birthday celebrations, and virtual cocktail hours with our families in front of our computer screen in an effort to stay connected in some way. It is amazing that we were able to continue to function and stay connected virtually. I can't imagine how much more difficult surviving the year would have been without this access.

However, what about the consequences of technology and the disconnection it can cause? Early in the pandemic, I would hear self-proclaimed introverts joke, "I've been preparing for this my entire life. I'm wired for this—to be alone and never leave my house." Yet just a few months in isolation and having most of our connections through a computer screen, the introverts, like many of us, had a very different story. It was painful, really hard, lonely, and mundane. The human deprivation during the lockdown shined a bright light on a problem that was already there.

Another death by 1,000 cuts. With each hour we spend on digital devices, we create another wound by taking time away from connecting, gathering, and listening. We are slowly eroding our relationships.

Like most of our problems—e.g., too much drinking, too much eating, too much spending—we tend to minimize or underestimate this one. It is a natural tendency as humans to deny how much we are doing something and the consequences of our behavior. Digital technology has become one of the biggest listening inhibitors, and I believe we are underestimating the problem. Listening is hard, and with the advent of digital technology, listening has gotten even harder.

We are bombarded with messages and things to distract us from people, especially the people we care about. Digital technology is like cigarettes, designed to make us addicted, to give us a quick fix, to wire our brains to want more. With all of its advantages, technology has become our biggest distractor and inhibitor, creating human disconnection. This side effect of digital technology makes listening more important than ever.

Ask yourself: Is digital technology interfering with my ability to listen and be present?

EXERCISE

Calculate and write down the number of hours you spent using digital technology today.

CHAPTER SUMMARY

1. Listening is hard. The subconscious is a superpower, the one in charge, in control. While listening, our subconscious is firing on all cylinders and telling us to do everything, except listen.

2. Listening inhibitors are things that interfere with one's ability

to listen. The three most common inhibitors are mind reading, rehearsing, and problem solving.

3. No one likes to be told what to do. Even though most of us are trying to be helpful by solving the problem, when we start telling, it leads to resistance.

4. Talking kills results. While listening gets us so much more of what we need to know than talking, too many of us spend most of our time talking and telling.

5. Digital technology is the big, new listening inhibitor. Adults in the US spend an average of seven hours and fifteen minutes a day on smart phones, desktops, and other devices watching content and engaging with online apps. Digital technology is a dichotomy. It has connected us in ways that were unimaginable, and at the same time, it is creating more disconnection than ever. Listening was already hard—with the advent of digital technology, listening has gotten even harder.

?

- Chapter 11 -

IDENTIFYING YOUR LISTENING PERSONA

"Silence sucks the truth out."

— CIA

L istening is hard. The subconscious is the enemy of listening and gathering a story. Many things are firing off subconsciously, telling us to do everything but listen. It's like wrestling an alligator. Inhibitors like trying to read others' minds and anticipating what the teller is going to say, or problem-solving and rushing to the solution run rampant. Or how about rehearsing, practicing what we're going to say next to respond to the teller? These are the things that are happening subconsciously.

Then there are things like just being in the habit of talking too much. And, of course, we're consumed by digital technology, which is distracting us from listening effectively. All of this makes listening a hard skill to build and master.

Unfortunately, there's still more to overcome. The subconscious has two listening personas. One is a helpful persona that gathers the story; the other is a huge obstacle. Most of the time, the un-helpful persona shows up—go figure. Hold tight. I'll tell you more about the two listening personas of the subconscious and how this plays out in a moment.

GETTING THE WRONG STORY

How would you rate yourself as a listener and your ability to gather the right story? When my team and I ask our audiences and clients, most people rate themselves as okay or a lit-tle above average. People also say they be-lieve they are far better listeners and better at getting the stories when they are focused on the task at hand. It goes like this: If I know I am supposed to be listening, I will listen more intently and be more intentional. Then I feel I am a pretty good listener, and I'll get the story.

Even the better listeners, including those who are both present and in-tentional, still fail at listening.

My EQuipt team and I set the bar higher. Our new paradigm and the gold standard for being a good listener is gathering the real story, uncovering or discovering the meaning of the story, or the insight, creating a connection, sharing the journey, and having the teller confirm that they feel understood. Do you know if you are getting the real story when you are listening? Do you know what you are missing? Do you think you shape the story the teller tells you? Here's what I have learned over many years of working with people: even the better listeners, including those who are both present and intentional, still fail at listening.

We do an exercise to show this very point. It always goes the same way, no matter who's in the audience or if we do this exercise with a handful or hundreds of people. This exercise came out of something very serendipitous. As we were developing our framework to transform how to listen, we were playing with the idea of what questions the listener should ask as they gather the teller's story—should they be able to ask anything they want, or should we give them some suggested questions?

Some fundamental questions—best practices if you will—exist, like the ones all journalists and therapists ask to get a story. The thought was: What would happen if we allowed the listener to ask only those fundamental questions and nothing else? While working with one of our clients, a well-known business school in the Philadelphia area, I decided to test it out and see what would happen via a large group exercise.

PEOPLE LEAD WITH THE PROBLEM, THE STRUGGLE

I described the exercise as follows:

Typically, when people tell you a story, they start with the problem, or the struggle, but only a part or piece of the problem. They usually don't start at the beginning or tell the whole story. They give you bits and pieces. I learned this from my counseling experience.

Specifically, one time I was working with a woman who came in for marital counseling. The woman, we will call her Beth, was a client of ours at the EAP and a high-level home shopping network executive in her early forties. Beth started her story by saying, "I need help with my marriage, but my husband refuses to come to therapy." I jumped right in and said, "We can certainly improve your marriage even if your husband doesn't join the sessions." It was important to get to Beth's real issues quickly since her benefits included only eight sessions with me.

After meeting with Beth three times, I thought we were making good progress. At the start of our fourth session, Beth told me something pretty important and relevant to the work we were doing together. She said, "Christine, I have something I need to tell you." Beth went on to tell me she was having an affair with her neighbor who was her husband's best friend.

Are you kidding me? I can't believe you didn't share this with me from the start! I did not say that out loud, of course, and went on with the session.

Afterwards, as I reflected, I realized it wasn't Beth's fault she didn't tell me this critical piece of her story sooner. I realized most clients I saw started with a piece of the problem, and it was up to me to earn their trust and ask the right questions to get the whole story. Clearly, I hadn't done either with Beth.

After telling this story, I asked the audience, "How many times have you been with a customer, an employee, your spouse, or your children, and they didn't start by telling you the whole story?"

With that introduction, I proceeded to explain the exercise we were about to do. The rules were: I'm going to tell you a story and your job is to gather my story. I'm going to start by telling you a piece of the struggle, the problem, and you are allowed to ask me any questions you want. I will answer any questions you ask, but

I will only answer the exact question you ask.

After I got confirmation that they understood, I began the exercise. Okay, here we go.

Christine: Here's my struggle. I was working with a mother and daughter, and the daughter punched the mother in the face. Now it's your turn. Ask me anything you want and gather my story.

Audience Member: Why did the daughter punch the mother in the face?

Christine: The mother said something flippant, sarcastic to the daughter.

Audience Member: What did the mother say?

Christine: I don't specifically remember the words, but I remember it was sarcastic.

Audience Member: How old was the daughter?

Christine: She was fourteen.

Audience Member: Was there violence between the mother and the daughter before?

Christine: No, this was the first time.

Audience Member: Was the father in the picture?

Christine: No.

Audience Member: Why were you working with the mother and the daughter?

Christine: I was their therapist. The daughter had conduct disorder.

Audience Member: What is conduct disorder?

Christine: It is a DSM V diagnosis. Basically, what it means is the daughter's conduct was out of control and she was at risk of harming herself, not necessarily directly but inadvertently. She was running away from school, getting into trouble, etc.

Audience Member: What was the mother's reaction to the daughter hitting her?

Christine: She was hurt both physically and emotionally. She was crying.

Audience Member: What was the daughter's reaction after she hit her mother?

Christine: She was remorseful immediately. She felt very badly. The mother and the daughter really loved each other. The daughter had frustration issues, and the mother and the daughter were more like siblings than parent and child. The mother was sixteen when she had the daughter.

Audience Member: What did you do after the daughter hit the mother?

Christine: I jumped up, got between them, deescalated the situation, and we got the mother some ice. We did a therapeutic intervention. They were fine. I was not.

BLAMING THE LISTENER

At this point, I hit the pause button and ask the audience how it is going. "How are you feeling? Are you getting my story?" I get several responses. "We're confused. We don't know what's going on." Or "We don't know the point of your story. Why are you telling us this? We are frustrated, and you're not being very cooperative. You're only giving us a little bit of information at a time." To which I respond, "Are you blaming me, the teller? So, it's my fault that you don't have the story? I said you can ask me anything you want, and I believe I have answered exactly what you've asked. Is this what you are going to say to your customer when they don't tell you about their problems, pain, and needs?"

On occasion, I even get, "Christine, are you the daughter? Did you hit your mother? Was that you?" To which I respond, "Okay, Dr. Phil, clearly we are watching too much TV, and you think there is some dramatic mystery to reveal. I know I told you I had a mom with psychological problems, but no, I'm not the daughter in this case." The audience usually laughs.

EXERCISE

Write down a time when you blamed the teller or when you were blamed as the teller.

_____

_____

_____

_____

THE DEFENSE ATTORNEY OR THE CURIOUS DETECTIVE

As we continue to debrief after the exercise, I put up a slide with a picture of a man dressed in a suit pointing his finger and looking angry. Next to him, I put up a picture of a man who looks like Benedict Cumberbatch. He is playing the curious detective, Sherlock Holmes, as he does in the series *Sherlock*.

I ask the audience, "As you collectively asked me questions to get my story, who were you, the curious detective or the defense attorney?"

The result is typically a fifty-fifty split. Then I explain that the defense attorney asks very specific and targeted questions, shaping the story they get from the teller on the witness stand to prove their case. This audience was not the angry defense attorney like the man in the picture, but it does happen....

Let me explain. I had a memorable experience while doing this very exercise with a group of nineteen executives at a large technology company. The executives became so frustrated by their confusion and what they perceived as my lack of answers doing this exercise that they upped the pace and tone of questions to the point where I had to stop the exercise. I was feeling like I was being interrogated and was getting a knot in my stomach. This is an example of how the angry defense attorney looks, as opposed to the kinder, gentler defense attorney.

Back to the debriefing. After we talked about how there are different types of defense attorneys, I continued, explaining that when we are gathering a story, the subconscious has two options, or personas, and the one that is usually in charge is the defense attorney. We hear a bit of information and start telling ourselves a story such as "Christine might be the daughter since her mom had psychological issues." Then we shape the story to fill in the blanks and either prove or disprove our case, rather than staying curious and open to what the teller is saying.

The defense attorney asks very diagnostic, specific, closed-ended, and factual questions. By contrast, the more helpful curious detective asks questions that relax the teller and allows the story to unfold. The curious detective creates an atmosphere of trust and the teller's defenses come down. With this new knowledge, I again asked the audience, "Which persona were you when getting my story?" They concurred that they asked factual, close-ended, and specific questions. While they were nice about it, they essentially interrogated me and could now see how, without even realizing it, they became the defense attorney as they gathered my story.

The university staff audience was genuinely interested in getting my story and getting it right, so they were very intentional in how they were listening. Their intentions were all good and even caring. They had no constraints, no restrictions on which questions they could ask—they were allowed to be curious. Unfortunately, even though they asked good questions, they were the wrong questions to get the right story.

I was only halfway through my experiment to prove we found a better way to get to the story, and I was excited about what would happen next.

Now that you know the two different listening personas, do you see how easy it is to become the defense attorney? How often does that happen when you are listening and gathering a story?

EXERCISE

Write down four examples of questions you asked in your last customer meeting or a meeting with an employee or colleague. Were those questions open-ended or diagnostic and specific?

_____

_____

_____

_____

CHAPTER SUMMARY

1. People tend to rate themselves as better listeners than they really are.

2. Even people who are good at listening, focusing on being attentive and intentional, still fail at listening.

3. The new paradigm and gold standard for being a good listener is gathering the real story, discovering the meaning of the story, and finding the insight.

4. When people tell us a story, they typically start with the problem, or the struggle, but only a part of the problem. It's up to

us as the listener to seek out and get the whole story.

5. The unhelpful listening persona is the defense attorney who asks very diagnostic, specific, closed-ended, and factual questions. The defense attorney shapes the story to fill in the blanks and either prove or disprove their case.

6. The subconscious has two listening personas: one is a helpful persona; the other is a huge obstacle to listening.

7. The more helpful, curious detective asks questions that relax the teller and allow the story to unfold. The curious detective creates an atmosphere of trust, and then the teller's defenses come down.

?

- Chapter 12 -

LOOKING FOR THE
MOONWALKING BEAR

"The best vision is insight."

— *Malcom Forbes*

E ven when we are very intentional and focused, it's very easy to fail at getting the story. So many obstacles can get in the way. The teller often starts with the struggle, the problem, in their story, which can create confusion without us knowing it, leading us to blame the teller.

Furthermore, the subconscious has two listening personas, the helpful, curious detective and the other persona that shows up more often: the less helpful defense attorney. Rather than being curious about the teller and their story, this persona asks very specific, closed-ended, and factual questions to fill in the blanks of the story that they shape in their subconscious.

As my team and I tried to figure out how to create a framework to overcome all these obstacles and help transform how people listen, we started thinking about the questions that therapists and journalists ask. Is it better if the story gatherer asks any questions they want? Or is it better to suggest a list of questions they could ask, perhaps the ones journalists and therapists use to get a story? Or, better yet, should we narrow it down to only six questions? We decided to experiment.

Getting back to the story in the last chapter, we had just completed the first half of the exercise and the audience had gathered my story by asking anything they wanted and me answering anything they asked, but only what they asked. This led to the audience asking all kinds of good questions to get my story, but it resulted in them feeling confused, frustrated, and not clear about what the story was or what the point was of me telling the story. As we debriefed, the audience realized they unintentionally ended up gently interrogating me by asking questions like a defense attorney, rather than being a curious detective.

QUESTIONING, THE OPPOSITE OF LISTENING

Have you considered how curiosity and asking questions can interfere with getting the real story? Doesn't that sound counterintuitive? The more questions we ask, the more we should learn about the story, right? I liken this to eating. Why is it that the more we eat over time, the hungrier we feel, and the more we want to eat? Shouldn't it be the more we eat, the less hungry we become over time?

Unfortunately, it doesn't work that way. Over time, the more we eat, the more our appetite actually goes up and the less we feel satiated. This is not dissimilar to what happens when we're gathering a story. Questions can create an insatiable appetite for asking more questions, which can derail both the gatherer and the teller.

GETTING THE REAL STORY

Now on to part two of the Story Gathering exercise where we test our hypothesis—when you limit the listener's questions, you get the real story faster and easier. I put up a slide with the following six "questions."

1. Take me back to the beginning?
2. Tell me more?
3. How does that make you feel?
4. Then what happened?
5. Hmm....?
6. It sounds like you felt *(fill in the blank)*?

These are the six questions journalists and therapists use. I then tell the audience we are going to do the same exercise, this time with a twist. Their job as a team is to gather my story. The twist— they are only allowed to ask me the six questions listed on the slide. They can ask the questions in any order they like, and as frequently as they like, but they can't add questions except filling in the blank for the last one. I repeat the instructions, and say, "Okay, I'm going to start with the struggle, here we go.

"I was working with a mother and daughter, and the daughter punched the mother in the face."

Audience Member: Tell me more.

Christine: We were sitting in a common area, and the mother said something flippant, sarcastic to the daughter, and before I knew it, the daughter had punched the mother in the face.

Then there was some hesitation from the audience. The room was silent. I waited. Then....

Audience Member: Can you take us back to the beginning?

Christine: I was twenty-five years old, working in a children's psychiatric hospital called the Philadelphia Child Guidance Center. It was an intense environment with a team approach. Most days I felt I was over my head. Sometimes I would have as many as twenty people watching me conduct a therapy session from behind a one-way mirror. We had a phone on both sides of the mirror and the head of my unit would periodically call in and give me specific instructions on what to say to the family.

Then I paused.

Audience Member: Tell me more.

Christine: I had just finished a session with the mother and her daughter and about twenty people behind the mirror. This was pre-HMOs, when hospital stays were thirty days. We had a classroom in the hospital, so kids weren't missing a month of school. I had a mentor who used to say the real therapy happens on the car ride home. We were finished with the session, and I was walking the mother and the daughter to the classroom (the metaphoric car ride home), so the unofficial therapy session continued. We had a few extra minutes, so we stopped at a common area and the three of us continued our discussion.

Audience Member: How did that make you feel?

Christine: I was feeling great, confident. I had performed well in front of a group of twenty people behind the mirror, and I was making therapeutic progress with a mother and daughter.

Audience Member: Then what happened?

Christine: The mother, daughter, and I were talking, and tension between the mother and daughter began to escalate. This was not uncommon in this environment, so I was feeling fine, like I had things under control. As things continued to escalate, I remember a nurse walking by who was probably twice my age. She said, "Christine do you need help?"

Audience Member: How did that make you feel?

Christine: I felt annoyed, and like the nurse didn't trust that I could handle the situation because of my age.

Audience Member: Then what happened?

Christine: Well, before I knew it, the mother said something sarcastic to the daughter, and the daughter turned around and popped the mother in the face.

Audience Member: What happened next?

Christine: I jumped up, got between the mother and the daughter. The mother was hurt, both physically and emotionally. She was crying. We got her some ice and did a therapeutic intervention. The daughter was remorseful right away. She had impulse and frustration issues. The mother and daughter really loved each other. They were fine, and we went back to the classroom. I, on the other hand, was not fine.

Audience Member: Then what happened?

Christine: Well, I held it together for the remainder of the work-day, but when I went home, I was a mess.

Audience Member: Tell me more.

Christine: I felt so responsible for what had happened between the mother and daughter. I felt responsible because it was my fault.

Audience Member: Tell me more.

Christine: I kept thinking about how the nurse asked if I needed help, and I didn't accept it. I thought she didn't think I could handle the situation because of my age. I was being stubborn. As I reflected on it, I realized I saw needing help as a sign of not knowing how to handle the situation and as a weakness, and because of my unwillingness to accept help, the mother and daughter experienced something awful. It was a very valuable, but painful lesson that I try to use as a reminder whenever I am hesitant or reluctant to accept help. Needing or accepting help is a sign of strength that can lead to better outcomes or avoid someone getting hurt.

EXERCISE

Think of a time when you used open-ended questions instead of closed-ended questions when gathering a story. What was the difference in outcome between the two?

_____

_____

_____

_____

FINDING THE INSIGHT

What is the difference between the first time the audience gathered my story, asking any questions they wanted, versus the second time, when the audience only asked the six questions that journalists and therapist ask? This is the very question I asked the university audience. The audience noted the first time they asked very specific and closed-ended questions. The second time, the questions were all open-ended. I then asked, "Did you get my story?" They said yes. Okay, then what was the insight in my story? What was the point? One audience member said it was that I realized asking for help was a strength, not a weakness. They added, "You try to use that lesson in your work whenever you hesitate to accept or ask for help." Exactly...do you see how using the six questions eliminates confusion and both the story and insight came to you as the gatherer?

To be honest, though, as I was in the midst of debriefing the exercise, I could barely contain myself; I was so elated. After seeing how things unfolded and hearing the audience's feedback, I knew we had unearthed something very powerful: to transform how we listen and get the real story, limit the questions to only six.

What happened next was even more incredible. Once again, our client taught us something even greater than we perhaps taught them. A woman said, "That was fascinating to watch unfold. What I saw was that the first time we gathered the story, all our questions were about the mother and daughter. The second time, by using only the six questions, it was clear the story was really about you."

I knew we had unearthed something very powerful: to transform how we listen and get the real story, limit the questions to only six.

That revelation seems so obvious to me now, but honestly, it hadn't occurred to me at the time. I was so focused on whether the audience would get my story by only asking these six questions that I missed the biggest insight of the experiment.

This woman got the bigger insight…the first time the questions were all related to the mother and daughter; the second time the story was all about me. She became the ultimate story gatherer, as she helped me discover something, a hidden gem, I didn't see. As she gathered the story of the Story Gathering exercise, she helped me realize something I would not have realized without her help. I learned again, first-hand, that when someone helps you see something you didn't see, it is game-changing and incredibly powerful.

DID YOU SEE THE MOONWALKING BEAR?

Have you ever had the experience of someone helping you discover something you didn't realize? How did that make you feel? How did it change you? How did it change your relationship with that person? To help people transform how they listen, we use the exercise we used with the university staff to help show that questions can lead to missing the story, the lesson of the story, and the insight.

I use a video I think helps to punctuate this point for our clients and workshop audiences. It's called "Awareness Test." Before showing the video, I instruct the audience just to watch and tell them we will debrief afterwards.

The video starts with a voiceover saying, "This is an awareness test. How many passes does the team in white make?" Then you see eight people on camera dressed like basketball players. One team has on white tops, and the other team has on black. Each team has a basketball, and while there are two distinct teams and two distinct balls, all eight are weaving in and out of each other as they pass their respective ball to their respective teammate.

As the video is playing, my team and I are again focused on watching our audience watch the video. What we see are people's eyes locked on the screen following the ball being passed by the team in white. After about fifteen seconds, the video stops, and the voiceover says, "The answer is thirteen."

We see participants either smile smugly in delight because they got the right answer or humbled that they got it wrong.

Then comes the big reveal. After a brief pause, the commentator adds, "But did you see the moonwalking bear?"

The video is quickly rewound for the viewer and restarts at the beginning. The video plays again, with all elements remaining exactly the same. However, this time the audience is looking for something different. This time, as the passes are thrown in the swirl of people, as obvious as the nose on a face, you see a man dressed in a bear costume, come into the middle of the shot, stop, do a silly dance, and then moonwalk out of the camera shot. The audience laughs, the majority flabbergasted that they missed something so obvious—this includes me the first time I saw it.

We are making great progress at this point in the listening transformation as evidenced by the answers and insights coming much more easily. As we debrief with our audience, we ask them what the point is and why we showed them the video. They tell us, "When you are looking for something specific, you can easily miss the most obvious and important thing."

I tell them the video was made as an educational traffic safety video showing drivers we can easily be unaware of cyclists on the road. We are not used to looking for things we are not accustomed to see on the road, so we can miss something obvious. The same is true when we gather a story. When we are focused on asking questions and filling in the blanks of the story, we can miss seeing what is obviously on the path.

EXERCISE

Describe a time when you were looking for something specific but missed the obvious.

_____

_____

CHAPTER SUMMARY

1. Questioning has a negative effect on listening. Questions can create an insatiable appetite and hunger for asking more questions, which can derail both the gatherer and the teller.

2. By limiting the story gatherer to asking only the six questions journalists and therapists use, the story and insight unfolds more naturally.

3. The six most powerful questions are: take me back to the beginning, tell me more, how did that make you feel, then what happened, hmm, it sounds like you felt (*fill in the blank*).

4. We should always be looking for the insight when gathering a story.

5. Insight is detecting something others don't see. It's incredibly powerful when the story gatherer helps the teller discover an insight. It creates a connection, trust, and foundation of understanding.

6. Our subconscious can miss seeing what is obviously on the path when we gather a story focused on asking questions and filling in the blanks.

?

FOLLOWING THE PATH TO UNDERSTANDING

"If you can't explain it simply, you don't understand it well enough."

— *Albert Einstein*

?

- Chapter 13 -

THE LISTENING PATH™

"If we can share our story with someone who responds with empathy and understanding, shame can't survive."

— Brené Brown

Listening is the most powerful form of communication—not talking, telling, or even storytelling. We at EQuipt have created a new paradigm and a better way to listen in a transformative way—Story Gathering is a process of moving from a one-way to a two-way journey, where the listener and the teller share the adventure and discover something that is hidden beneath the surface. That is, they discover an insight that leads to something better. As my team and I developed the process of Transformational Listening, we had to figure out how to simplify a difficult and complicated skill so anyone could transform how they listen.

We figured out a big piece of the puzzle when working with a well-known university in Philadelphia. More of the story is uncovered by limiting the number of questions the listener asks the teller. This results in the curious detective emerging naturally in the subconscious. We knew we had unearthed something very powerful, yet so simple.

The next step was to create a framework that marries all the needed tools together, including those six journalist questions, so the listener can gather the story, uncover the insight, and change the conversation. We call this framework the Listening Path. I am going to introduce you to the five tools in the framework one-by-one and show you how to use them on the path. Using the tools separately is helpful. Marrying them together transforms how you listen.

TOOL 1: THE LISTENING PATH

Do you think in pictures or visual stories? Neuroscience proves that we remember stories ten to fifteen times more than we re-member facts. When I learned ten years ago that I am dyslexic, I also learned that I make sense out of complicated things by turning them into pictures in my mind. To help you transform how you listen and use the tools, I'm going to give you the gift of my dyslexic brain and create a mental picture that you can visualize as you are Story Gathering.

Imagine that you and a friend have decided to go on a backpack-ing trip. Each day, you have a certain number of miles you need to hike to arrive safely at camp before you run out of daylight. While you are an experienced backpacker, your friend is new to it, so you will serve as the guide throughout the journey.

What do you need to take with you so you don't get lost? Well, of course, first you need a map of the path or trail. When do you turn left instead of right? How do you ensure you are not getting confused about where you are going? How do you know which direction to head and where the steep parts are? Without a trail map, you will struggle to find your way, and it will take you longer to accomplish your goal.

The same is true when you are gathering a story. You first need a map of a story's path to ensure you know where you are going and can safely guide both you and your friend.

STOPPING ON THE PATH

What is on the Listening Path map? Picture a dirt path in the woods. The path starts out on a flat surface and, as the trail turns, you descend into a ravine where the trail is difficult, and you are uncertain. After the ravine, you make your way up to a mountain peak. Finally, you make your final climb of the day to your destination. You pass four important milestones or stops on the trail to help keep you oriented. This is key—when you as the listener know where you are on the path, you are able to guide the teller and get the real story without getting lost.

Here's a bonus. Those who consider themselves to be highly impatient listeners or have difficulty paying attention will get the story much more quickly than before. One time I had a workshop participant say, "It used to take my wife nine hours to tell me about her nine-hour day, and I didn't have that kind of time or patience." His intonation was telling. I couldn't resist saying, "Let me guess—you two aren't married anymore?" He laughed and said, "Nope." The other workshop participants laughed as he was expressing what many of us feel—it's hard to be patient and pay attention when someone is talking, even someone we care about. Just like backpacking, you and the teller get to the destination faster when you follow the path.

STOP 1: THE BEGINNING

Do you ever feel impatient when you are trying to listen? Do you want to get the story faster? So, where do you start? Let's follow Maria von Trapp's advice in *The Sound of Music* and start at the beginning, the first milestone or stop on the Listening Path. When gathering a story, getting the beginning of the story is one of the most critical parts in ensuring we are setting out on the right course.

Just like a movie, when we don't know the beginning, it's difficult to get our bearings and figure out where the story is going. The beginning includes the background, the scene, the character(s), and when and where the story began. The beginning holds many clues to who the story is about, who needs the help, and the insight the story holds. Without starting at the beginning, the story gatherer will inevitably get lost.

EXERCISE

Think of the last time you tried to help someone solve a problem—did you get the beginning of the story? Write down the first thing you gathered.

_____

_____

_____

_____

_____

_____

_____

STOP 2: THE STRUGGLE

Have you ever thought about how much of a story is about the struggle? The second milestone or stop, the struggle, is the most significant part of the story. Here's why…just like when you set out to backpack on an unfamiliar trail, when you gather a story, there are struggles and problems that the teller, like the back-packers, have faced along the way. In fact, the struggle is actually the most important part for the listener to gather and understand.

It's like a movie. Think about it. Most of a movie is about the struggle. Once we understand the setup, the characters, and when and where the movie began, the rest of the movie focuses on the struggle. It doesn't matter if it's an action movie, a com-edy, or a drama. Most of the movie is about the problems the characters face, what it costs them, and who's affected.

This mirrors the discovery process in sales. If we are doing it right, our meetings with potential customers are mostly about discovering their problems, pain, and needs. Getting to this mile-stone on the path is critical to success because it is where all the drama lies and where we can be part of the solution.

STOP 3: THE TIPPING POINT

What does it mean to have a tipping point? How much does reaching the tipping point matter in a story? Milestone or Stop 3, the tipping point, is the shortest stop on the path. This is where change happens. The characters in the story have had enough of the problems, stress, and drama and are ready to change to overcome the obstacles.

The tipping point is what has happened that leads the character to change. For example, Mary has been smoking cigarettes since she was thirteen. While her health is affected, it's costly, and her husband and friends hate that she smokes, she hasn't been motivated to stop. Tipping point: Mary and her husband are trying to have a baby, so now she has a reason that motivates her to make the change.

When gathering a story from a teller, the story sometimes already has the tipping point; other times, the tipping point hasn't yet happened. Distinguishing this is the secret to figuring out if someone is ready to act, opt in, or buy and how to help move them to the next milestone.

STOP 4: THE NEW BEGINNING

Why "the new beginning" instead of the end? Don't stories and movies have endings? Endings are traditionally how storytellers have thought about how to wrap up a movie or story. I believe there are few endings to stories. Instead, each story leads to the start of a new beginning. Think about the example of the woman who found her motivation to stop smoking because she wanted to have a baby.

Milestone four on the path is the new beginning. It is what life is like once she has stopped smoking. What's different? What's the outcome or the result? How does she and her friends and family feel once she has stopped? Her story didn't end—she just set out on a new course. How about you and your friend on the trail? At the end of the day of backpacking, you get to your destination and set up camp for the night.

It's the end of the day, but it's the beginning of the rest of your journey. Just like the tipping point, as the story gatherer, you need to know that the teller may not have their new beginning figured out just yet. For example, the story I told about the woman from the university workshop who helped us discover something that led to a new beginning at EQuipt. Her insight that the story was about *me*, not the mother and daughter, affected the trajectory of EQuipt's story, helped us set a new course, and became a powerful influence. The same will be true for you.

FACTS AND FEELINGS

Did you know there are two other essential things to understand while you are on the Listening Path to gathering a story? They are facts, of course, and yes, feelings!

It's easy to gather facts, as the tendency is for the defense attorney listening persona to show up with that insatiable appetite for more facts. We start firing off all kinds of questions eliciting more facts—let the interrogation begin. Here's a very important point. If we only gather the facts and don't gather the feelings, we miss understanding the most important part of the story—the person we are gathering the story from, the teller, the character. As we travel the path to gathering the story, we need to get more than just the facts. We need to find the feelings along the way or we miss the person.

> **If we only gather the facts and don't gather the feelings, we miss understanding the most important part of the story—the person.**

Do you now have the picture of the Listening Path, the map, painted in your mind? Can you see the path, the four milestones or stops, and the facts and feelings you need to gather along the way? The backpacker knows not to try to wing-it to figure out where the trail goes. They start the journey with the tools they need to get to where they are going.

Do you see how visualizing the path will help you know better how to guide the teller? The experienced backpacker uses a map as a visual guide to where they are on the trail to ensure they don't get lost. When they have done it long enough, they become a kind of trail guru. I consider myself a listening guru, if you will. In creating the Listening Path, our goal was helping our clients, but an unexpected and wonderful outcome was that I have also helped myself become an even better listener.

As experienced as I am as a listener, like the experienced back-packer, I'm even better when I'm not winging it. By visualizing the path, I always know where I am when gathering a story, and if I'm feeling confused, I know it's time to pause, reorient, and ensure that the teller and I don't get lost.

EXERCISE

Explain an instance when you had to gather both facts and feelings to understand the teller. What happened?

_____

_____

_____

_____

_____

_____

CHAPTER SUMMARY

1. The Listening Path framework has all the tools you need to gather the story and uncover the insight. Five tools are included in the framework. While using the tools individually is helpful, combining them transforms how you listen.

2. As we go on the Listening Path, we imagine we are backpacking, hiking a path with the teller. You are the guide to getting the teller's story.

3. The first Listening Path tool you need in your backpack is the map of a story's path to make sure you know where you are going.

4. The four stops, or milestones, on the path are:

   Stop 1: The beginning, including the background, the scene, the character(s), and when and where the story began. The beginning holds many clues to who the story is about and the insight it holds.

   Stop 2: The struggle is the problems and obstacles the teller has faced on their journey. The struggle is the most important part of the story for the listener to gather and understand.

   Stop 3: The tipping point is the shortest stop on the path. This is the moment when change happens. The characters in the story have had enough of the problems, stress, etc.

Stop 4: The new beginning shows us what's different, the outcome, the result of the story, and the new beginning of the teller's journey.

5. On the map are both facts and feelings; it's important to gather both. If we merely gather facts, we miss understanding the most important part of the story; the person we are gathering the story from, the teller, the character.

?

- Chapter 14 -

USING THE SIX MOST POWERFUL QUESTIONS

"Effective questioning brings insight, which fuels curiosity, which cultivates wisdom."

— Chip Bell

Transformational Listening is a very complex skill. However, if you stay on the path, we've made it simple by creating a framework that gives you all the tools you need to gather a story. We call this the Listening Path. To review briefly, the first tool is the path itself, the visual map, that serves as your trail guide for gathering a story.

The path has four milestones, or stops: the beginning, the struggle, the tipping point, and the new beginning. You will need to find all four milestones as you gather a story. Along the path are both facts and feelings that need to be discovered.

While the facts will be the most natural to seek out, seeking out the feelings is crucial as well. If you don't seek out the feelings, you will miss the most important part of the story, the person, the character. As you listen and gather the story, imagine the picture of the path in your mind.

The path will keep you oriented as to where you are in the story, ensure you and the teller stay connected, help you avoid getting lost, and lead you to the point or insight of the story.

It's time to give you the second tool, the six most powerful questions. These should sound familiar because we discussed them back in Chapter 11.

TOOL 2: THE SIX MOST POWERFUL QUESTIONS

Now that you have your first tool, the map of the path, loaded into your backpack, what else will you need to help get to your destination?

While I'm not an experienced backpacker, I have a team member who is. His name is Dean, so we asked him. He said the map is only good if you know which direction you are going, so it's also helpful to have a compass because it's really easy to get turned around, especially if you aren't experienced in the woods.

Well, that makes sense, doesn't it? The second tool on the Listening Path is the six questions. These questions are your compass. The questions, used by master story gatherers, good journalists, and therapists, easily point you and the teller to where the story needs to go.

Let's take a look at each of these questions to better understand why and how they work.

TAKE ME BACK TO THE BEGINNING?

As we discussed in previous chapters, we either meet people in the middle of their life's movie, or people start with a piece of their problem, their struggle, rather than the beginning of a story. If we don't have the context, the beginning, we are inevitably confused about who and what the story is about, which sets us off on the wrong course.

A key to getting to your destination faster is to slow down to speed up. One of the best ways to do this is to ask the teller to take you back to the beginning or just take you back. Think about it, when we take a step back, we get a much better view of things.

I often say we don't go to the Philadelphia Museum of Art to stand six inches from a Monet. We need to step back six feet or more so we can see the big picture and not just the fine brush strokes. The beginning of the story gives us the bigger picture; as we continue on the path, we will get the brush strokes, the fine details, the facts and feelings that shape the story.

"Take me back" is a very powerful request. Asking someone to do this differentiates you as a listener because you are slowing the teller down, making sure you understand their beginning, and laying the groundwork to uncovering the insight.

How many times have you been listening to someone tell you a story and, near the end, a critical detail comes out that if you had known sooner, would have helped the story to make a lot more sense? Commonly, what is our response? "I can't believe you didn't tell me that sooner." Remember what the high-level executive told me in session number four? We blame the teller for not giving us the whole story, whereas it's our responsibility as the story gather to make sure we have all the parts. Many of us are not good storytellers, so setting up the story and making sure the listener has it all is not a common strength.

More importantly, when we gather a story from someone who doesn't know us, or where the teller is feeling vulnerable, we need to guide them to trust us. Building trust and finding the early clues of the story are usually done at the beginning. Be sure to ask the teller to take you back to the beginning.

THEN WHAT HAPPENED?

How many times have you asked yourself this question in your subconscious? Our subconscious has a pretty big appetite for wanting to know what is going to happen next. The simplicity of this question verbalizes to the teller what your brain wants to know. Rather than shape the story by adding onto the question, just ask it in the pure form.

For example, you're gathering a story from your colleague who just had to fire someone. They say, "I decided to fire Pat." Rather than ask, "What happened after you decided to fire Pat," simply ask, "Then what happened?" If you ask the first, more specific question, you elicit a specific answer, which may essentially steer them to give you more facts that could be insignificant to the story.

Instead, when you ask what happened next, you leave it open for the teller to tell you what is important or significant to them, which is much more revealing. You hear what happened next that mattered to the teller, rather than what matters to you.

HOW DID THAT MAKE YOU FEEL?

How do you feel about asking this question? I believe you're feeling, "I'm not sure I feel comfortable asking that question. That is not a question I would ask someone in a business conversation." I hear this all the time from clients and audiences. Here's what I find so ironic about these concerns. When I introduce the question, the first thing I ask is how people feel about asking it. Funnily enough, people don't hesitate to tell me exactly how they feel—uncomfortable, uneasy, like it's too personal a question, especially in business.

We are discussing how uncomfortable the question is to ask, yet we don't get resistance from people about answering it. That's what's so fascinating about the "How does that make you feel?" question. It's the most powerful question most people don't notice you've asked.

We are human, and humans feel. We feel in our personal lives, and we feel in our business lives. We don't head out to work in the morning saying, "I am going to leave all of my feelings at home today. I don't have any feelings about work, coworkers, customers, profits, and/or success."

"How does that make you feel?" question. It's the most powerful question most people don't notice you've asked.

That would be crazy, right? We all care about our work, our success and failures, the people we work with, and why we do what we do. We all have a one-word passion, even if we haven't yet developed the language to articulate it. For the teller, sharing their feelings is a natural thing to do. You just have to ask them.

There are a few things to keep in mind about this question that I think will help you overcome the struggle of asking it. First, how you ask the question—your intonation—has a lot to do with how it is received. If you are conversational and comfortable asking it, then the teller will be conversational and comfortable answering it. Remember we talked about mirror neurons? Asking comfortably will take some practice, but pay attention and I promise you will see it is easy to do.

Second, I've asked this question in nearly every business meeting or conversation I've had since starting my career. No one has ever said, "How dare you ask me how I feel!" The worst thing that has ever happened is that the person hasn't answered, but again, I promise, this is incredibly rare.

I had one of these rare instances just a couple of weeks ago with a client I've worked with for thirteen years. I called to follow up on a referral he was making on our behalf. During our short conversation, he told me a member of his leadership team had resigned unexpectedly.

I paused and asked, "How are you feeling?" He started to answer and then said, "I'd like to talk with you about this in person rather than on the phone." My takeaway was that this was too important for a quick phone conversation, not how dare you ask me how I feel.

Third, when you ask people how they feel, you make an unconscious connection with the teller. This is a caring question that shows the teller you care about how they feel and how they are affected, which builds trust.

Finally, if you are impatient and want to get the story more quickly, ask how the teller feels. Ironically, we tend to ask about facts, yet facts get you and teller stuck in a bit of a rabbit hole and off the path. Feelings move the teller and the story along. Watch what happens when you ask someone how they feel, and you will see that the teller moves forward and opens up more about both the facts and feelings. The meaning of the story lies in the feelings, not in the facts.

EXERCISE

Write down how you feel when you think about asking someone how they feel in a business conversation.

_____

_____

_____

_____

TELL ME MORE....?

Have you ever noticed anyone making this request? Pay attention because it happens more often than you think. Like the question, then what happened, this request taps into the subconscious' appetite for knowing more. The problem is we are wired to take this powerful, open-ended question and ruin it by saying something like, "Tell me about blank," and we fill in the blank with the facts we are chasing.

For example, "Tell me more about why you decided to fire Pat," or "Tell me more about what he did after you fired him," and so on, and so on. When we ask someone to tell us more about a certain thing, it means our defense attorney is lurking and we are shaping the story we want the teller to tell us.

Keep it simple and pure—just ask them to tell you more, and I guarantee your subconscious will relax, and your curious detective will appear.

HMM?

Are you thinking, that's not a question? Again, you're not alone. In the written form, hmm becomes a question when you add the question mark. When you say it, you can just add a slight intonation to make it a question. I said earlier that as much as 93 percent of communication is non-verbal, including intonation. Hmm is an example of a subtle and almost imperceptible question. When someone is really listening and gathering well, you will notice them subtly say with a slight nod of the head, "Hmm?" It's just a natural thing that happens.

Several years ago, I was working with a large technology company's chief customer officer (CCO) and his leadership team. Like many do, he was struggling with how asking these six questions could be helpful to their business. His office is responsible for resolving complicated problems that happen when customers implement the company's technology. The CCO and his team have to understand their customer's problems deeply and identify a way not only to fix issues but to get the customer to overcome their frustrations and lost confidence. They have to regain lost trust and credibility.

As we were doing a practice Story Gathering exercise, a senior vice president (SVP) from the CCO's team was sharing a real customer story, starting with only pieces of the struggle. The CCO was the gatherer, getting the story using only the six questions, while the SVP was the customer with the problem, the teller. The CCO was staying true to the process, but it was evident he was out of his comfort zone. The exchange between the SVP and the CCO naturally moved from a practice exercise to a real-life business conversation, which is common.

I could see the CCO was relaxing and becoming more comfortable as the Story Gathering went on. Then there was this great moment. The SVP said something about how he felt and, in response, the CCO very authentically leaned in and uttered, "Hmm?"

I saw all the other team members notice what happened as result of the question. I decided to immediately stop the exercise and debrief to capture what the team saw and felt. They said they noticed how that simple hmm further connected the CCO and the SVP and, without effort, the teller kept going with more of the story.

The CCO also had an epiphany. He said, "Our team has to be empathetic to our customers' feelings, not just solve their problems. When we just listen and gently ask and guide them to share their story, we will start to earn their trust back." From that day forward, he directed his teams to ask only these six questions on their first meeting with customers.

IT SOUNDS LIKE YOU FELT _____?

Do you feel better saying this than, "How does that make you feel?" People often tell us this feels a little easier. This is the only time you get to fill in the blank. It sounds like you felt...angry, stuck, upset, frustrated. It sounds like you felt...elated, thrilled, relieved. The beauty is it doesn't matter if you get the feeling right. It only matters that you ask.

For example, if you say to the teller, your coworker, "It sounds like you were upset that you had to fire them?" using intonation to change the statement into a question, your coworker isn't going to say, "I can't believe you thought I was upset, not even close! Either you're a bad listener or you clearly don't care about me;

otherwise, you would have gotten it right."

Instead, they will simply clarify by saying something like, "No, I wasn't upset. I was actually relieved. They were not working out. We had a lot of conversations about performance and how I could help, but they came to realize the job wasn't for them. Firing someone is never easy, but Pat thanked me for all I tried to do. We gave Pat a package so he will have a little time to find a more suitable job. I'm actually feeling quite relieved."

The result of this statement bent into a question is you will know exactly how the teller feels, and you will also learn a lot more about the story itself.

RUSHING TO THE END

When you are listening, do you ever find yourself trying to rush to the end of the story? This is a very common problem. That darn defense attorney wants to confirm or shape how the story ends. The big part of the problem is that many stories are about struggle and pain. Seeing or hearing that someone is in pain can make us feel uncomfortable and urge us to create a storybook ending.

Rushing to complete a difficult story has happened to me, as I am sure it has with you. For example, when I tell someone I was in acute pain and basically disabled, facing multiple surgeries for almost ten years after a car accident, guess what the very next statement usually is?

"You're doing better now, right, Christine?" That's a beeline from a piece of my struggle directly to a storybook ending. I certainly understand the desire to hear the happy ending after hearing about my struggle. One of my therapists, Perpetua Neo, reminded me that, as the listener, the greatest gift to give is to bear witness to the pain. This is where empathy is born, so rather than rush to that storybook ending, try saying, "Tell me more," or "It sounds like you felt..." and then name the feeling.

This will allow you to bear witness and give the gift of true empathy. You receive an even greater gift because the teller will never forget how you made them feel.

EXERCISE

Explain a time when you felt rushed to finish your story. How did that make you feel?

_____

_____

_____

_____

LESS IS MORE

Are you asking yourself, "Are these the only six questions I will ever use when I am gathering a story?"? The answer is, of course, no. However, let me suggest a few things.

First, the more you practice using just these six questions, the more you will learn that you get more with them than with all the other specific questions your defense attorney is forming.

Second, the ratio of questions should be no less than three to one. Use one of the six questions three times more often than one specific or targeted question. This is a guaranteed way to stay on the path together and not get lost by wandering onto too many side trails.

Finally, asking fewer questions allows you and the teller to get to the story faster.

IMPROVISING INSTEAD OF READING THE MUSIC

Okay, I'm going to get on my soap box a little here, so please bear with me. I get a little frustrated when people want to improvise before they learn the questions in the purest form. Could I ask the question this way instead? I understand it's uncomfortable to try something new, but I liken this to someone who is learning to play the piano.

Unless you are a natural or can play music by ear, you won't be able to play a song until you first learn the notes. You need to master the notes of a song before you can improvise and play it your own way. Most of us are not natural listeners. The second tool, the six questions, are the notes of the music. I speak from experience when I say it takes discipline to learn something difficult.

I decided to learn how to play the piano when I was unable to play sports after my car accident. Never did I swear more than when I played from my piano book *Teaching Little Fingers to Play*. Oh, the irony of my R-rated language playing music from a book for five-year-olds. The last thing I wanted to do was stick to the music and the fingering as outlined on the page.

My left brain was going wild, and I thought I'd never get it. Of course, I was wrong. I just needed to stay true to the process and stick to the notes. Before I knew it, I was using both hands and could put together a simple song.

ONE IS BETTER THAN NONE

When you are on the path, it works best if you use all six questions. Use the questions like you are sewing together different pieces of a garment. As when making a garment, you can start with one piece at a time. First, practice adding just one question until you master using it. Start with, "Take me back." Use that in your conversations as you gather a story.

Practice and become comfortable with it; then add another. Perhaps try, "How did that make you feel?" or "Tell me more," and so on. Each time you add another question, observe what happens. How did the teller respond? Did they open up and tell you more, or did they shut down? Did you get to the story faster or slower? Observing the feedback and the result of your efforts is the best way to ensure you will use these questions. I will guarantee the effect and the results will be powerful.

Do you see how using the six questions helps you get the story more easily and efficiently? The questions are your compass on the path. Listening is hard. We know that the subconscious is a beast and can be the enemy of getting the story. Listening inhibitors like mind reading and rehearsing distract us and take us off the path.

We also have the story we are telling ourselves and the defense attorney working against us. Remember how fortunate I was to have coaches who knew how to get me in shape without me thinking about running? They made sure we did drills with a ball so I wouldn't have to think about the miles I was putting in.

These six questions are so powerful because they metaphorically serve as your ball. The questions distract your brain from all the other noise, quieting the listening inhibitors and the defense attorney. You're able to listen without thinking about what you are doing, getting you in shape and transforming your abilities along the way.

EXERCISE

Write down an instance when you have used one or more of these questions. How did it shape the conversation?

_____

_____

_____

_____

_____

_____

CHAPTER SUMMARY

1. The second Listening Path tool to put in your backpack is the six most powerful questions that master story gatherers, journalists, and therapists use. These questions serve as your compass to ensure you and the teller stay on the path.

2. "How does that make you feel?" is the question people object to asking because it feels far too personal to ask in a business conversation. Most people don't notice you are asking about their feelings; they just appreciate that you care enough to ask and will tell you more.

3. Asking the two feelings questions gets to the teller's story faster. Feelings open up the teller to sharing more of the facts and the story.

4. "Take me back" is a very powerful request. As you gather, you slow the teller down, ensuring you understand the beginning of their story.

5. Asking, "Then what happened?" leaves it open for the teller to share what is important or significant to them, rather than you shaping their story by asking about what is important to you.

6. Saying, "Tell me more" allows your defense attorney to relax and your curious detective to appear.

7. "Hmm?" is an example of a subtle and imperceptible question. When someone is really listening and gathering well, you will notice them subtly verbalize and with a slight nod of the head, say "Hmm?"

8. "It sounds like you felt elated, thrilled, relieved." It doesn't matter if you get the feeling right. It only matters that you ask.

9. You will find using just these six questions gets you more of the story than asking specific and pointed questions.

?

- Chapter 15 -

REFLECTING IN THIRTY TO NINETY SECONDS

"Most people do not listen with the intent to understand; they listen with the intent to reply."

— *Stephen R. Covey*

The second tool on the Listening Path is the six most powerful questions, which are: Take me back to the beginning, Then what happened?, How does that make you feel?, Tell me more, Hmm?, and It sounds like you felt _____. These questions act as your compass as you travel the path. They quiet the defense attorney and the listening inhibitors that distract you, disconnecting you from the teller and taking you both off the path. All these questions are powerful individually.

However, when you use them together and refrain from using others, you become the ultimate curious detective guiding the story so it unfolds naturally and almost effortlessly.

Of all the questions, the one people seem to struggle with seeing the relevance for in a business conversation is, "How does that make you feel?" The objection is typically that it feels like that is far too personal to use in business and the most uncomfortable question for people to ask.

To transform how we listen, we need to get over this discomfort and realize we are all human and humans feel. Regardless of whether we are at home or at work, we feel all the time. It's not a faucet that turns on and off. Additionally, business is very personal and evokes many feelings. Seeking to understand the feelings of the teller is the only way to get the real story and will get you to the problem, the point, the insight, and ultimately the result, faster.

Now that you know how to gather a story by using the path, which is the map to the story, along with the six questions, which are your compass, it's time to introduce you to the third tool. This tool, the thirty to ninety second reflection, is the first step to ensuring that you and the teller are completely aligned in understanding the story.

TOOL 3: UNDERSTANDING IN THIRTY TO NINETY SECONDS

Have you ever thought about the last time you agreed to something with someone and left the conversation convinced you were completely aligned? Perhaps it was with an employee where you shared the top priorities or a directive about a project. You believe you were crystal clear about what you asked them to do, they agreed with what you asked, but somehow a week later, you found out they did something in complete contrast to what you believe you said and discussed. As a result, you are frustrated, you've lost some confidence in your employee's ability to take direction, or their ability to understand the priorities, and you have lost a week. In full disclosure, I've made a decent amount of money over the years by helping sort out this kind of problem.

While I could have continued to make a living this way, I'm not interested. I kept having the same conversations over and over again, taking an individual approach to what I knew was a systemic and organizational problem. This was contrary to both my nature and training.

Once I figured out how to close the gap of misunderstanding, I started to address the problem systemically and create a path for all to follow. Communication between two or more people is complicated, but I assure you we are making the problem harder to fix than it has to be.

We rarely confirm that we are aligned around a common under-stating. Instead, we wait for the communication to fail and then conjure up a story to explain why it didn't work out. For example, "I told my employee what I needed them to do; they didn't do it. My employee doesn't understand the priorities. I'm losing confidence in them."

The thirty to ninety seconds reflection is the third tool to put in your backpack for your hike on the path. For the sake of the metaphor, we will call this your flashlight so you can shine a light on what you are getting and what you are missing as the story gatherer.

Communication between two or more people is complicated, but I assure you we are making the problem harder to fix than it has to be.

After gathering the story from the teller, the gatherer spends thirty to ninety seconds reflecting what they heard. Just by virtue of knowing that it is your responsibility to reflect the story you heard in thirty to ninety seconds, you will pay closer attention to the teller. The reflection tool raises your awareness and helps you to be more present. The reflection tool also ensures you, the gatherer, have heard both the content and the meaning of the message or story.

Be patient with yourself. It takes some practice using the tools to let them do the work for you. At first your subconscious will remain in overdrive, but in time, the tools will allow you to quiet your defense attorney so you can be present and able to get all of the story. Not to worry; it will come, and knowing what you need to reflect will help you as well.

EXERCISE

Think about a time when you reflected a story, or someone reflected your story. How did that change the conversation or the outcome?

_____

_____

_____

_____

SIFTING THE STORY ON THE PATH

What do I need to reflect? How do I pare down a ten-minute discussion to ninety seconds or less? I was recently watching Stephen Colbert conduct an interview. The guest, the teller, gave Colbert a long answer to a pretty short question. Colbert laughed and said, "Okay, I just got out my sifter," and while making the gesture of sifting something, said, "I'm going to sift what you just said."

Colbert then reflected the highlights and meaning of the guest's longer answer in two sentences. I remember thinking, *That is a brilliant metaphor for reflecting. It's sifting out the important ingredients so they blend together into the meaning.*

FOUR STOPS

How will you know what is important and what to reflect? The path helps you reflect just like it does when you gather a story. Use that picture of the path; conjure it up in your mind, including all the milestones or stops. Picture what the teller said in the beginning, then the struggle, then the tipping point, and finally, the new beginning. One by one, reflect each milestone on the path and share the highlights you heard.

From one milestone to the next, weave together the story you just heard. Interestingly, while you were the story gatherer, as you reflect you become the storyteller, honing this skill as well.

FACTS AND FEELINGS

Is it hard for you to hear and reflect feelings? When gathering the story, initially it is much easier to seek the facts and miss the bigger opportunity to ask the teller about how they feel. The same is true when reflecting the story.

It's fascinating to observe our clients learning to gather because they quickly get pretty good about asking about feelings, despite their initial objections. By asking the two feelings questions, the gatherer gets all this good stuff. Asking the feelings questions uncovers meaningful things about the teller, and we observe a different level of connection between the teller and the gatherer unfold in front of us. It's as if only the gatherer and the teller are in the room, even though they are in groups of five or six.

What happens next is pretty common. During the reflection, the gatherer leaves out all or most of the emotions and feelings they just got the teller to share with them. They gathered an emotional and meaningful story and scrubbed out the person, the connection, and the feelings. It's interesting to watch the teller's reaction to this because it provides many lessons for the teller, the gatherer, the observers, and my team.

While there is an inherent politeness, you can see the teller is disappointed and feels misunderstood since the gatherer left out the emotions. The connection that was developed quickly starts to evaporate.

One time when we were working with a leadership team based in New York, the CEO, who was German, told a story about firing his best friend who had brought him into the company. The CEO was not only sharing his emotions, but he also said things like, "I was devastated; it was so painful," etc.

He was also exuding emotion as he told the story. He got teary at one point, looking pained. While the gatherer reflected all the stops on the path, she was devoid of emotion. The CEO politely listened without much expression. As we debriefed after the exercise, I asked the CEO how he felt. He said, "I can't believe she didn't reflect anything I felt—it was as if a doctor was diagnosing me."

Ironically, the woman who gathered his story said, "I didn't think you were comfortable with me asking about or reflecting your emotions." I said, "Tell me more." "Well," she replied, "he's German, and I perceive him as uninterested in emotions." The story she told herself about his interest or comfort with emotions based on his German heritage ultimately interfered with her hearing the emotions he was clearly sharing both verbally and non-verbally.

This was a very interesting lesson. We learned how the stories we tell ourselves interfere with us listening, and most importantly, the negative impact on the teller, in this case feeling diagnosed.

DETAILS MATTER

What about the facts and the details? How much should we reflect? This is a delicate balance and, again, you will need to be patient with yourself because it is a matter of practicing to get better and better at finding the balance. Initially when people try the thirty to ninety seconds reflection, they tend to do one of two things. One, the gatherer repeats, almost verbatim, every detail, both factual and emotional, which leads to it feeling more like a recording of the words than a reflection of the story. Two, the gatherer gives such a high-level reflection that it doesn't have enough detail to make sense of the story.

A guide I have found very useful is to think about the reflection like this: If someone told me a story and someone else walked in the room, I should be able to catch the new person up in ninety seconds or less. I should be the storyteller who shares the story in a way that the second person has everything they need, including the four stops, the facts, the feelings, and the meaning with enough detail that the first person doesn't need to say a word.

DOING THIS INTERFERES WITH UNDERSTANDING

What shouldn't you do when you're reflecting and gathering? First, what inevitably happens as the teller is sharing their story is your subconscious reminds you of an experience you've had. Your brain starts to take you in a different direction, thinking about your experience, how you related, and that you and the teller have a lot in common. This is a blessing and a curse.

The obvious blessing is we have a lot more in common with people than we know because we live above the water so much of the time and don't look below the surface. Stories help us go deeper. The curse is that your subconscious will want to pull you into talking about your experience rather than staying focused on the teller.

You will be tempted to jump in and share your experience, to relate to the teller, but it's important to wait, finish the gathering, and reflect first. Otherwise, you divert the conversation to being about you instead of them. Listening is a gift, an unselfish act, that leads to better things, but timing is everything.

The second "don't do" when gathering and reflecting is to rescue the teller from their feelings. As we discussed in previous chapters, bearing witness to the pain of others is listening's gift, but it can be uncomfortable, to say the least. This came to life in a compelling way when we were conducting a workshop with a company in Rhode Island.

The company is a medical advocate benefit company for employees of their corporate clients. The staff is comprised of doctors, nurses, and social workers—notoriously compassionate people by profession. We were practicing Story Gathering and the ninety-second reflection in a breakout session. A woman in her early forties was talking about how her career kept her away from home and how that affected her five-year-old daughter. She described how things came to a head one morning when her daughter had a complete emotional meltdown.

As the woman told this part of the story, I could see she was going back in time and reliving the pain of that experience. Then she started to cry.

As soon as the tears started to flow, the group of eight, even though there was only one official story gatherer, jumped into action to try to console the woman. One whipped out a tissue, another tried to give her a hug and tell her it was okay, while another made a joke to try to make her laugh.

In mere seconds, they all swarmed her to help her feel better. All I could see was how much the woman wanted to keep sharing her story—she needed to keep going. Sharing the story is part of how we heal and forgive ourselves for the mistakes we make.

I ended up doing something I rarely do. I threw out my arms like an official calling a foul and very firmly told everyone to stop. Then I took over the gathering as if nothing had happened. The woman continued with her story, as if nothing had happened as well. In the end, she told us that even though it was painful, ultimately, she was grateful for the terrible day because she realized her daughter needed her more than her work, so she decided to change her priorities.

Bearing witness to someone's pain isn't easy for anyone, but it particularly wasn't for these highly compassionate professionals who just wanted to make her feel better in her moment of pain. When gathering, it's important to let the feelings be felt, and by reflecting, acknowledge that you heard them.

Have you ever found yourself feeling uncomfortable when someone shows emotions? It's okay if you feel uncomfortable. Focus on reflecting the story instead of solving the problem, and you have taken another step toward transforming how you listen.

EXERCISE

Have you ever had someone trying to listen to you as the teller end up diverting the conversation away from you? How did that make you feel?

_____

_____

_____

_____

CHAPTER SUMMARY

1. The third Listening Path tool to put in your backpack is the thirty to ninety seconds reflection; we call this tool the flashlight. It shines a light revealing that you and the teller are completely aligned in your understanding of the story.

2. After you gather the story, and when you think you have it all, spend thirty to ninety seconds reflecting what you heard.

3. To reflect, picture what the teller said at all four stops on the

path. One by one, reflect each milestone on the path and share the highlights, reflecting both facts and feelings.

4. Reflecting takes some practice; it will not come naturally at first. The goal is to sift through both the facts and the feelings, repeating the story in a way that anyone can understand.

5. You will relate when gathering the teller's story. You will be tempted to jump in and share your experience and tell your story to connect. Timing is everything. Be careful not to divert the conversation from the teller to you. Stay on the path of gathering.

6. It is easy to reflect only the facts and leave out the feelings. It is critical to let the teller's feelings be felt by reflecting and acknowledging that you heard them. This creates connection.

?

Chapter 16

AFFIRMING UNDERSTANDING

"Nothing in life is to be feared, it is only to be understood."
— *Marie Curie*

The third tool on the Listening Path is your flashlight, the thirty to ninety seconds reflection. This is the first of two steps of confirming true understanding between you and the teller. More often than not, communication between two or more people is an exchange of telling and rarely an exchange of what was heard or understood. We walk away from our conversations assuming we are aligned and understand each other without validating that understanding was the actual result. We all know the saying about assumptions...when you assume, you make an ass out of you and me.

This assumption leads to a lot of problems, including misalignment, misunderstandings, con-

> **More often than not, communication between two or more people is an exchange of telling and rarely an exchange of what was heard or understood.**

flict, disconnection, wasted time, wasted resources, and more. This is a silent epidemic in all relationships, whether it be a twenty-five-year marriage or a first sales call with a potential customer. It takes practice to stay on the path and learn how to sift all the story ingredients so we can reflect it correctly, much like when we sift the ingredients to bake a cake.

When we blend the right mix of facts, details, and emotions into our reflection, we blend the right ingredients to ensure understanding and meaning. This shines a light on the story so we can take a second step confirming we understood. Without this, we remain in the dark.

Now that you've reflected the story, the second step is to affirm your reflection. That is, to confirm your understanding of both the teller and their story. The fourth tool on the Listening Path is an affirming phrase.... Do I get you?

This affirmation is the life blood of true understanding, much like water is the life blood to backpackers on a long journey.

Since the backpackers can't possibly carry enough clean water to sustain them for their entire trip, they have to filter their water along the way to ensure it is free of contaminants. Similarly, when we are on the path to gathering a story, the subconscious contaminates both what the teller says and what the gatherer hears.

We need a filtration tool, and "Do I get you?" is the affirming phrase we use to ensure we have eliminated the contaminants and gained a pure understanding of the teller and their story. This is the only way to keep our relationship hydrated and healthy along the journey.

TOOL 4: AFFIRMING

Are you wondering why the phrase, "Do I get you?" Maybe you're thinking, "That just sounds weird. I don't think you understand, Christine. I would never say anything like that." Let me start by saying, "I get you." The reason I'm confident I get you is I remember having the same initial reaction.

Let me take you back.... I first became aware of this question in 2011 when I met Mike Bosworth, the creator of Solution Selling. Mike was famous in the sales world for changing how salespeople sold and won deals with his methodology starting at Xerox in the '70s. I was introduced to Mike by one of his lifelong friends, Marv Perel. Marv had worked for Mike early in his career and has a forty-year successful sales career ranging from large technology companies to smaller entrepreneurial ventures.

I met Marv by happenstance when we were at a mutual friend's wedding. I have been fortunate to work and collaborate with Marv over the past ten years, and I credit him with helping me reach a new understanding in solving the problem of what it costs not to listen, starting with introducing me to Mike.

Marv is incredibly curious and interested in others. That is why he has been largely successful throughout his sales career.

Marv learned about my background in psychology and emotional intelligence at the wedding and thought Mike would like me to read the draft of his latest book on the power of storytelling, *What Great Salespeople Do*, and provide feedback. I thought Marv was kidding, of course, but sure enough, a day later, the draft was in my inbox.

I was very impressed with what Mike wrote and created, not only because of how he approached selling with storytelling, but even more so because he recognized the importance of listening and empathizing with the buyer.

Mike wrote about the phrase "Do I get you?" and why it is so powerful. He talked about the difference between situational awareness and personal awareness. "Do I get it?" implies situational awareness on the part of the listener. I, the listener, understand your situation. "Do I get you?" implies personal awareness. I, the listener, understand you and your situation, both personal. Furthermore, Mike said, "Personal awareness can have a much greater impact on a meeting than situational awareness."

Why is this the case? Brain science has proven that the emotional brain lights up when we buy. Understanding the buyer's emotions in this case helps you sell. More simply put, as Marv says, "Sales is simply a transfer of emotions."

Many people feel more comfortable saying "it" or "your situation" instead of "you" because it removes the emotional language. So why was I struggling with this phrase? It certainly wasn't because I didn't like asking or discussing the emotions—quite the contrary. As I reflected about what was getting in my way, I realized that I felt conspicuous as a former therapist.

I felt like saying "Do I get you?" was too obvious of a way to let someone know I wanted them to feel understood emotionally. My initial reaction was that it is too in your face. I certainly didn't want clients, colleagues, and friends thinking I was trying to be their therapist, especially in light of my professional training.

Then I remembered my earlier training at the Child Guidance Center and the power of using exact words. As a young therapist, I had worked with a family while being observed by a team behind the mirror countless times. The protocol was that if the team had a directive, the supervising therapist would be called into the room. I would pick up the phone and the supervisor would give me the exact words I was to say to the family. This was not optional; you were to say things exactly as instructed. If I didn't follow through on the directive, I would get another buzz on the phone. If I was still struggling, I would be asked to come behind the mirror to discuss why I was stuck and how to overcome what was getting in my way.

All of this was not just for my benefit; it was also to provide the best help possible to and for the families we served. When I was given the exact words to say, my inner dialogue was often, "Holy shit! I can't say that. That's too direct, doesn't sound like me, and/or are you kidding? The family is going to go ballistic!"

Thankfully, we were held accountable and also given a lot of support to help us overcome whatever was making it difficult to use the exact words and we were coached on how to be effective. I learned over time that the worst never happened when I said the exact words I was given, and, conversely, that when I did, change happened.

The words the supervisor instructed me to say were very intentional. Why should I say them exactly as I was instructed? Because they worked. The supervising therapists had decades of experience saying things that were far less effective and had figured out the most powerful ways to get to the heart of the matter quickly. Words matter, and exact words matter. Mike had already figured out the exact words to connect to the buyer faster, so I started using the exact words. Again, no disasters. Quite the contrary, just like asking "How does that make you feel?", no one seemed to notice, and the results were powerful.

Mike and I had been working together for almost two years when I told him I needed to go off on my own to truly demystify transforming how we listen. I was grateful for both his mentorship and support. "Do I get you?" is a powerful phrase. When you marry those words with the rest of our Listening Path tools, the game changes.

LISTENING FOR UNDERSTANDING

Are you willing to experiment and say "Do I get you?"? See if anyone notices or what your friends', customers', or spouse's reaction is. I can assure you that you won't be disappointed by the results and, before you know it, you'll be reflecting in ninety seconds or less and saying, "Do I get you?" in the most conversational way.

EXERCISE

Explain how you can incorporate asking "Do I get you?" into a conversation with a friend, family member, or partner.

_____

_____

_____

_____

Okay, so then what happens? Let's play this out a little bit so you know what to expect. The conversation from this point goes one of three ways.

SCENARIO 1

You gather the story using the path; reflect in ninety seconds or less, sifting through the emotions, details, and facts; and then say to the teller, "Do I get you?" The teller gives you a bit of a mixed answer. The words the teller says, their verbal communication, is yes. However, their non-verbal communication and intonation is no. As story gatherers, we too often focus on the words rather than seeing if the words and the non-verbal cues match.

A slang phrase found in the Urban Dictionary explains this yes-no answer from the teller. Brace yourself…the phrase is "Grin-fucked." The Urban Dictionary describes grin-fucked as, "In business, when someone smiles and shakes your hand, assuring you that they have heard and will act upon your recommendation or concerns when in truth you have already been ignored and dismissed." The grin (the verbal answer) is, "Yes, you get me." The fucked (the real answer beneath the surface) is, "No, you don't get me at all, but I'm not going to tell you that."

How many times has this happened to you? For example, you're having a disagreement with your spouse; you go back and forth, and then you ask if things are resolved. You get a verbal yes, but they really mean, "Fuck no, this isn't resolved." The good news is when you have truly taken time to gather the teller's story, reflect, and affirm if you get them, the yes-no mixed answer is usually provoked out of politeness, rather than something negative. The teller sees that you have made the effort, that you care about them, and therefore, doesn't want to push back on your reflection because of the effort you made.

We often see this play out in our workshops when participants practice the Listening Path tools. The gatherer gets to the reflection and the affirmation, "Do I get you?" The teller doesn't want to discourage the gatherer, so they politely and not so convincingly verbally agree. The teller says something like, "Yes, mostly," with an accompanying shoulder shrug. The gatherer gets the verbal yes and a non-verbal no.

While this is the less common of the two scenarios, I raise this as a cautionary tale. Be sure to pay attention to both the teller's verbal and non-verbal cues when you reflect and affirm you get them. Otherwise, you may end up in the Urban Dictionary and miss the opportunity to uncover the real story.

SCENARIO 2

You gather the story using the path; reflect in ninety seconds or less, sifting through the emotions, details, and facts; and then say to the teller, "Do I get you?" The teller doesn't answer yes or no. Instead, the teller can't wait to clarify what you didn't get, what you missed, and/or tell you even more about the facts, story, and their feelings. It's as if missing some part of what they said somehow opens up the floodgates to even more of a dialogue, connection, and understanding.

Matt, a team member at EQuipt, whom I introduced you to in Chapter 8, started working with us after being a client. He had been incredibly successful in sales since he was sixteen and started a mobile vehicle detailing business in his neighborhood. Within a year, Matt was making $7,000 a month and was able to help his single mom go from working three jobs to just one. This was just the beginning of Matt's sales career. Matt and I met at one of the CIO forums where I was the keynote speaker in early 2019. He was intrigued by the Listening Path and asked for our help on some deals he was working on to learn how to apply the tools.

We learned that Matt's success was no accident. He was dedicated and a quick study. Once introduced to the Listening Path, he used every sales call, meeting, and conversation as an opportunity to practice the tools and transform how he listened. If you spoke with Matt today, he would enthusiastically share stories of how the Listening Path changed conversations with his customers and accelerated the buying cycle.

Matt also figured out something on his own regarding reflecting the story. He said, "Christine, sometimes I intentionally miss on what I reflect back to the teller and then say, 'Do I get you?' I have found that when I leave out an important detail or feeling, the teller is more inclined to affirm if it is as important as I thought it was by how they respond. As a result, I am able to understand even better and more quickly how to prioritize their needs and goals."

SCENARIO 3

The teller genuinely and convincingly affirms you got them.

GETTING IT ALL

What's next after you've reflected and affirmed with the teller by asking "Do I get you?"? In any scenario, it's important to go back to the beginning of the path, gather what you missed at all four stops—both facts and feelings—and reflect the story again. This time include what you missed and reaffirm, asking once again, "Do I get you?" Stay on the path until the teller affirms both verbally and non-verbally you got them. Trust me; whether you succeeded or not becomes very apparent as you practice this cycle a few times. Giving people the space to clarify and share more about how they think and feel is so powerful. Why is this?

I believe the world thirsts to be heard and understood. Much like the backpackers on the trail who need to stay hydrated, clean water is what sustains life and productivity on the trail to accomplish the goal. My experience is that people are woefully underhydrated when it comes to being understood.

I believe the world thirsts to be heard and understood.

Too few people are present, aware, and take the time to know and understand more about another and their story. When you listen to understand, you give the teller clean water. This earns trust and bonds you together so you can overcome obstacles and achieve goals together.

THIRSTING TO BE UNDERSTOOD

How often do you feel people really take the time to listen? Do you thirst to be heard and understood? I was reminded people thirst for being heard when I entered the online dating world after my divorce. For anyone who hasn't had an online dating experience, it is filled with a myriad of emotions and confusing tales. Lots of people tell you all their horror stories, including stories of being ghosted after the first date.

My experience was good early on in my post-divorce dating life, and I wondered what all the hubbub was about. I had a lot of success getting asked out on a second date and was never ghosted. My conclusion was, "Well, Christine, aren't you fabulous? The men you are meeting really seem to like you."

After a series of first and second dates, it dawned on me that my dates weren't asking any questions about me. Then my self-proclaimed fabulousness turned into, "Duh; it's not me they like. They like the way I make them feel."

I realized because I was such a good listener, gathering and reflecting my dates' stories, that they were loving the experience I was creating for them. They weren't getting to know me; they were asking for a second date because I was listening, reflecting, and affirming that I got them. This is a very powerful and rare gift, especially when meeting new people. Since I was ultimately uninterested in someone who wasn't interested in getting to know me, I decided to conduct a little experiment.

I intentionally dialed back on being such a good listener on the first date. I made a point to talk about myself, at times even interrupting to share more about myself. I still listened, of course, but also made sure there was more balance in the conversation. Interestingly, the result was that I didn't get as many second dates.

I came away with a couple of lessons from this experience. Getting so many second dates because of my fabulousness was a story my subconscious was telling me, not at all the reality. More significantly, it is great to show up and be interesting, but nothing makes a person more interesting than if they are truly interested.

SAYING YOU UNDERSTAND

Have you ever thought about whether the people you like to hang out with are more interesting or interested? Do they find a balance of talking and being curious, interested and truly understanding who you are or what you are going through? I have become even more maniacal in recent years, studying and watching how people talk and listen to each other.

The words "I understand" have very little to do with understanding and certainly nothing to do with the teller feeling understood.

One thing that stands out is how often the words "I understand" are used. The words "I understand" have very little to do with understanding and certainly nothing to do with the teller feeling understood.

When someone says they understand, my experience is that the gatherer is looking to end the conversation, change the subject, and/or start talking about themselves. It's one way the conversation gets out of balance.

How do you feel when you are talking with someone about a problem and their response is, "I understand"? Do you feel understood? I recently came to a tipping point in realizing how frequently people say the words I understand to convey understanding.

One of our clients is the head of the high school and student experience at a very affluent private school in Florida. She wanted me to help her and her leadership team learn to handle difficult conversations. The latest issue they were facing was that they couldn't hold the senior prom in the usual venue due to COVID restrictions. Wait for it.... The high school head went on to say in an understandably frustrated tone, "The parents are upset because the prom is being held on a yacht instead of at the country club as it is every other year." As she described the problem, I could see her team was equally frustrated by this being an issue.

I said, "Okay, let's role play. I'll be the parent," and I picked one of the leaders to be the story gatherer. I proceeded, playing out the dialogue of entitlement as they were used to hearing from the parents. The team member was gathering my story, well actually, as I was ranting. She sincerely said, "I understand," and then went on to explain further why they didn't have a choice.

I then stopped the role play, and we debriefed as a team. I asked the gatherer to take me back to when she said, "I understand," and how she quickly started talking about the logical reasons they couldn't accommodate the demand to have the prom at the country club.

As we processed, the team member said, "Come on; this isn't a real problem." I responded, "Well, it's a real problem for this parent. I get you. In the big scheme of things, this may not feel like a real problem to you, and I can only imagine how exhausting this must feel. If I had the means to give my kid a fancy country club prom and they were losing out on that experience, it would be hard as a parent that I couldn't give that to them."

As I reflected both the team member's and the parent's feelings, I could see the collective lightbulb go off among the team. When the team member said, "I understand," what she meant was, "It's time to move on to why we can't accommodate your demands," not "I understand how you feel." It is understandable that the team was having difficulty understanding the plight of these parents being so upset over having the prom on a yacht with the myriad of issues they were navigating with COVID.

However, understanding is not about agreement; it's about recognizing what it would feel like from the parent's perspective and reflecting that perspective. Even when it seems absurd, for the gatherer to keep both you and the teller on the path, affirming true understanding is key. The words "I understand" are lip service to understanding and just another example of how you end up in the Urban Dictionary and guarantee you will create a thirsty teller.

EXERCISE

Explain a time when someone said "I understand" while you were storytelling. How did that make you feel? How did that question affect the rest of your conversation?

_____

_____

_____

_____

CHAPTER SUMMARY

1. The fourth tool on the Listening Path is affirming understanding. The filtration tool "Do I get you?" is the affirmation used to ensure we have eliminated the contaminants and have gained a pure understanding of the teller and their story.

2. "Do I get it?" implies situational awareness. "Do I get you?" implies personal awareness. Personal awareness is much more powerful than situational awareness.

3. As story gatherers, we too often focus on the words rather than seeing if the words and the non-verbal cues match.

4. "Do I get you?" is a powerful phrase. You change the conversation when you combine the words "Do I get you?" with the rest of the Listening Path tools.

5. When affirming with the teller by asking "Do I get you?" if the teller doesn't affirm that you did, go back on the path, and gather what you missed. Then reflect again and reaffirm "Do I get you?" Stay on the path until the teller affirms both verbally and non-verbally you get them.

6. The words "I understand" have very little to do with understanding and nothing to do with the teller feeling understood. Affirming true understanding is key.

?

Chapter 17

MINI-REFLECTING

"There is more to hear in what is not said."

— Joyce Rachelle

We live in a world where the exchange between people is most often talking and telling instead of listening and understanding. It is far too rare for someone to be truly present and take the time and interest to understand someone's story. People are thirsting to be understood.

The fourth tool on the Listening Path is affirming by asking "Do I get you?" This affirming acts like the water filter backpackers use to ensure they have fresh water. When you affirm with the teller that you get them, you are affirming not only the teller's situation, their story, but also their feelings and emotions. You're also making sure your own story isn't contaminating the teller's story. You go beyond

> **We live in a world where the exchange between people is most often talking and telling instead of listening and understanding.**

277

the words "I understand" to express understanding. While understanding may seem obvious, it is often missed when listening.

We assume we've come to a common understanding since both the teller and the gatherer had an exchange. This fallacy leads to a lot of costly problems in both our work and personal lives.

Now that we have shown you the four primary Listening Path tools so you can take the teller on the path with you, including the map, the six questions, the thirty to ninety seconds reflection, and affirming with "Do I get you?" we are ready to weaponize your Story Gathering.

The fifth and final tool on the Listening Path is the mini-reflection. When two backpackers set out on a hike, they will inevitably go at different paces and temporarily disconnect. To ensure they don't get too far apart, or wander off on the wrong trail, they plan to check-in frequently and ensure they are following the same path.

The same is true with the teller and story gatherer. At times, one will get ahead or behind the other while they are on the path. The mini-reflection is a check-in to ensure they stay together and walk in each other's footprints to follow the trail together to the new beginning and insight.

TOOL 5: GUIDING THE TELLER ALONG THE PATH

How do you use a mini-reflection to ensure you and the teller stay together on the path? You may be asking, as the listener, "I thought I wasn't supposed to interrupt the teller when they are talking?"

Even though many of us interrupt people all the time, we usually feel badly when we do so intentionally. The reality is that to transform how we listen, we have to guide the teller on the path, slow them down, and help them stay on the trail, all without shaping their story.

Interrupting to talk or ask relentless, specific, or factual questions is a no-no. However, gently interrupting the teller to ensure you understand is an important part of being an amazing story gatherer.

I, too, used to consider it rude to interrupt people when they were telling a story or talking even though I was guilty of doing so. I learned how powerful and necessary it is to interrupt, or pause, the teller when I began training to be a host for Executive Leaders Radio (ELR).

One of the first things that struck me was how much the founder of the show, Herb, interrupted the guests, especially as we were conducting a practice interview in the green room. ELR CEO interviews are only ten minutes, so we have the guests keep their answers short to get as much of their story as we can. I watched how Herb and the rest of the hosting team asked the guests a question; then the guest would often go off on a tangent at length, talking about something unrelated to the original question. We wouldn't have many listeners if we didn't interrupt the guest to get them back on track.

> **That's what happens when we share our stories. We find so many small side trails that it's easy to get lost in the woods. We need a guide to ensure we don't get lost.**

That's what happens when we share our stories. We find so many small side trails that it's easy to get lost in the woods. We need a guide to ensure we don't get lost.

Watching Herb in action showed me the importance of interrupting, and why and how to interrupt or pause the listener. When you use the fifth Listening Path tool, mini-reflection, you interrupt the teller to slow them down. This creates a pause, ensuring you are walking at the same pace, staying together, and conveying empathy and understanding along the way.

STUDYING GREAT LISTENERS

I've always believed much can be learned simply by studying what others do well. As a public speaker, every time I watch someone give a presentation or speech, I study what they are doing to captivate the audience. I figure it's much easier to replicate what they are doing and merge it into my own presentation style than try to invent something on my own.

For the past decade or so, I have been a fan of *The Howard Stern Show* on the radio. Stern had a reputation for being outrageous and even rude, but he speaks often about how when he joined satellite radio he no longer had to be as provocative. Stern explained that he realized in his terrestrial radio days he was outrageous to stand out. Once he joined Sirius XM and could ask anything he wanted, he no longer had anything he needed to prove.

The kinder, gentler Howard Stern of Sirius XM Radio is grounded in deep, meaningful conversations that help his audience really get to know his celebrity guests. Many people say being on the show is the best experience they've ever had because of the experience Stern creates for them.

I've listened closely during my many hours of driving over the years and really studied Stern. Not surprisingly, he uses the six questions—Tell me more, Then what happened?, How did that make you feel?, etc.—as foundational interview questions.

As great as that is, what really makes Stern such an incredible story gatherer is that he regularly slows the pace of the interview. Guests tend to rush past the little known, yet important moments that they take for granted. Stern, almost with excitement, interrupts the guest and says something like, "Wait, wait, hold on a second—take me back to that moment. What did that feel like?" After the guest answers, Stern says something like,

"So, you're telling me...." Then he reflects the highlights of their answer.

Stern interrupts, goes back, and then affirms both the facts, the details, and the feelings by mini-reflecting. He reflects while he and the guest are on the path, rather than waiting until the end of the interview. The result of his mini-reflecting is that Stern guides the guest, the teller, and slows them down so not only he and the audience understand the story, but the guest sees the power in their own life moments and finds new insights. Often the guest will say, "I never thought about that."

Stern is conversational in his approach to both the questions he asks and the pace at which he interrupts to mini-reflect. He creates an amazing experience for his guests and the listener and is worth emulating. We are left feeling that we really got to know these famous, successful people and all the critical moments they went through to become who they are.

EMPATHIZING THROUGH THE STORY

Have you ever observed someone you see as a great listener? Have you studied or tried to emulate what they do? What did you notice? If you pay close attention, you will notice they tune in and reflect the emotions and feelings of the teller all along the path of their story. You will also notice that the listener reflects what isn't said by the teller.

What the hell does that mean? As your subconscious relaxes and your curious detective emerges, you start to gather the verbal and the non-verbal answers to get the real meaning of the teller's story.

We had a participant, we will call him Bob, in one of our workshops who shared a story that took place some twenty-five years earlier when he was a young officer working on a ship in the navy. One night while on duty, Bob's captain ordered him to take charge of navigating the ship while he went to bed. Bob told his captain he did not feel at all prepared to take charge of navigating the ship.

The captain said, "Bob, that is an order." Bob adamantly repeated his concerns, but to no avail. The captain repeated, "That is an order." At this point in the story, the gatherer gently interrupted Bob and mini-reflected, "It sounds like you were ordered to do something you felt unprepared for or didn't have enough experience to handle?"

While the gatherer was accurate in his reflection and was miles better than most listeners, he still missed what wasn't said. What the gatherer didn't pay attention to was the look on Bob's face when he said the captain gave him the order.

Bob had a look of absolute anguish and terror on his face. Yes, Bob felt ill-prepared. What he wasn't expressing with his words he overtly expressed with his face. His expression was telling of the depth of Bob's emotions and foretold the rest of his story.

The gathering continued. Bob went on to say that while he was at the helm, he misjudged the channel as he approached a bridge. He described a hair-raising scene, including how he hit the bridge and people almost lost their lives because of his inexperience and this mistake. It became obvious this had been a devasting experience for Bob and explained the look of anguish on his face earlier when he had recounted how the captain ordered him to take control of the ship.

The emotions Bob verbalized were that he felt he was ill-prepared and inexperienced; Bob's non-verbal expression was one of anguish and terror.

The mini-reflection allows the gatherer to slow the conversation down so there is time and awareness to gather both the verbal and non-verbal messages. If we only reflect what is said, we miss an opportunity to understand on a much deeper level and uncover what is going on below the surface. When we go beyond the words and reflect the depth of the emotion someone feels—what's not said—we create an unbreakable bond of trust all along the path.

EXERCISE

Have you tried to verbalize through non-verbal expression? If so, how did the listener respond?

_____

_____

_____

_____

TRANSFORMING HOW YOU LISTEN

Do you see how being able to hear what isn't said and mini-reflect along the path transforms the relationship between you and the teller? Would you like to give the gift of understanding the deeper meaning and emotions to your employees, business partner, customers, or children? What would it mean to them and to your relationship?

As you practice using the five tools of the Listening Path, you will see how the mini-reflection tool takes you from a competent to a great listener—metaphorically speaking, from a good singer to an amazingly inspirational virtuoso.

Mini-reflecting allows the story gatherer to be the true guide on the path, slowing the teller down and ensuring both are following the same path and not getting lost on a side trail in the woods.

HELPING OTHERS SEE WHAT THEY DON'T SEE

How will you know when you have the teller's story? How do you know you've gotten it all? Remember, the four milestones or stops on the path. Also remember, not everyone has reached the tipping point or new beginning of the story yet. Mini-reflections help the gatherer and teller know where they are on the path. By reflecting and confirming along the way, a clear understanding emerges as to whether the teller has reached a tipping point and found a new beginning.

Finding the insight is at the root of Transformational Listening.

As you gather the story, you are always looking for the insight, the meaning, something that others don't see. Sometimes the insight leads to the tipping point and a new beginning, and sometimes the insight is found buried in the full story. Mini-reflecting helps you know where the teller is on their story path.

Finding the insight is at the root of Transformational Listening. Listening is a way to help the teller discover something, to find a solution or an answer, using your eyes to help them find it. Insight means helping others see what they don't see and detecting unstated needs. Using all five tools together on a Listening Path allows the insight to find you.

IT'S NEVER ABOUT THE SHOES

We had an amazing example of insight coming to light right before our eyes a few years ago while conducting a workshop for a sales team at a digital marketing company in Chicago. At the end of day one of our workshop, we ask participants to practice the Listening Path tools that evening by gathering a story from someone they care about. We instruct them to use only the six questions, along with the other four tools, to gather the story and see what happens.

Furthermore, we tell them that one of two things will happen. One, as they gather the story from someone they care about, they will get a strange look and their loved one will say, "What are you up to?" We warn them that means they suck at listening. And two, we tell them, "You're going to have a transformational conversation." Finally, we instruct the participants to come prepared to share the story of their experience Story Gathering with the class the next day.

With the group in Chicago, we started the second day with a debrief of the homework. It was a particularly special morning. We had the usual "What are you up to?" stories. But we also had some amazing stories about transformative conversations. One particular conversation stood out because of the insight the gatherer had gained.

A participant, Jeffrey, raised his hand and said, "I gathered a story from my eleven-year-old nephew last night." Jeffrey was about thirty, single, with no kids, and an infectious smile that lit up the room. He said he called his nephew and started the conversation by saying, "How was your day?" His nephew said, "Not good." Jeffrey said, "Tell me more." His nephew said, "I didn't get the basketball shoes I wanted." Jeffrey said, "Take me back to the beginning," and "How did that make you feel?" His nephew said, "It made me mad. My dad promised he would take me to get new basketball shoes, but he never showed up."

As Jeffrey continued his story, he said his nephew went on to say his dad breaks a lot of promises these days. His parents are going through a rough divorce, and his dad isn't reliable like he used to be. Jeffrey said he and his nephew had a thirty-minute conversation talking about what it is like when your parents are going through a divorce, and what it has been like for the nephew, including how he was feeling.

At that point, we were all crying. Jeffrey's teammates were mesmerized by the connection Jeffrey had made during his conversation with his nephew.

Then Jeffrey broke the seriousness by saying something pretty funny. He said, "Christine, I'm mad at you." I responded, "Mad at me? Tell me more."

Jeffrey said, "This homework exercise cost me 150 bucks. I promised my nephew I'd buy him the shoes."

The room erupted in laughter, and I felt relieved. Then Jeffrey said something very profound. He said, "Christine, I also learned something really important from this exercise."

"What's that?"

Jeffrey said, "I learned, no matter who you're speaking with, it's never about the shoes."

That was way beyond insightful. Jeffrey understood that when gathering a story, people share the surface problem, not the deeper problem living below the surface. Very often people don't know what lies below the surface, or they don't feel safe enough to share the deeper meaning and feelings.

Jeffrey's nephew presented the problem that he didn't get the basketball shoes. The deeper problem was that his parents were getting divorced and his father was not as reliable as before and broke promises.

By uncovering the insight that his nephew wasn't upset about the basketball shoes, Jeffery took the relationship to a higher level. The difference between attentive listening and Story Gathering or Transformational Listening is uncovering the insight and what the story is really about.

EXERCISE

Describe three times when you used mini-reflections and how doing so changed the conversation.

_____

_____

_____

_____

CHAPTER SUMMARY

1. The fifth and final tool on the Listening Path is the mini-reflection; this is the check-in that ensures the gatherer and the teller are following the same trail and staying on the path together.

2. Sometimes either the teller or the gatherer will get ahead or behind on the path. The mini-reflection ensures they don't get lost in the woods.

3. Interrupting is necessary when Story Gathering. The difference is you are not interrupting to talk, but to mini-reflect. This slows the teller down, keeps them on the path, and prevents you and the teller from getting lost, all without shaping their story.

4. When studying great listeners, you will notice they slow the teller down by highlighting and reflecting moments within the story.

5. Mini-reflection allows the gatherer to reflect the feelings of the teller and empathize along the path to the story.

6. Pay attention to both the verbal and non-verbal messages as you gather. An unbreakable bond of trust is built when the gatherer goes beyond the words and reflects the depth of the emotion the teller feels.

7. Always look for the insight as you gather the story. Using all five tools together on the Listening Path allows the insight to find you.

?

- Chapter 18-

BEING SUCESSFUL IS NOT AN ACCIDENT

"Success is a process, not an event."

— *Gary Halbert*

The Listening Path provides you with the proven tools to shift from attentive listening to Story Gathering or Transformational Listening. That is, it allows the story gatherer to uncover hidden gems or insights and share understanding with the teller. Like backpackers hiking the trail, it's important the listener and the teller stay connected on the path, checking in to be certain they are following the same trail—staying on the same path and not getting lost in the woods on the way to their destination.

Mini-reflections are the check-ins between the teller and the story gatherer as they travel the Listening Path en route to the insight of the story and shared understanding. The ability to mini-reflect along the path is transformative because it opens you to hearing what is said *and* not said. This is game-changing.

We at EQuipt have made the process of Transformational Listening simple.

Please don't be misled by that statement—simple is not the same as easy.

SIMPLE VERSUS EASY

When was the last time you tried to learn something new, something that was out of your comfort zone or your natural abilities? What did it take to get really good at it?

Simple is defined in the *Oxford English Dictionary* as: basic and uncomplicated in design. We have made Story Gathering simple by virtue of design. You will become a highly skilled story gatherer by synchronously using the five Listening Path tools and sticking with the process.

Now let's define easy. The *Oxford English Dictionary* says, "Easy means without great effort or presenting few difficulties."

My experience is that most worthwhile things are not easy. Here are just a few examples: being married, raising children, managing employees, growing a business, serving your customers so they are satisfied, etc. A simple system or process is at least 50 percent of the solution, but doing what isn't easy, overcoming an engrained habit, is the other 50 percent. It takes effort and commitment to struggle through difficulties. Adding simple to doing what is not so easy is the only certain way to master something new.

EXERCISE

When was the last time you tried to learn something new that was outside of your comfort zone? What was it like for you?

_____

_____

_____

_____

ALL SYSTEMS ARE NOT EQUALLY HELPFUL

As I'm sure you have figured out, playing sports has been a life-long passion of mine. It was devastating for me to give up sports at thirty-one due to the injuries I sustained in my car accident. After a ten-year process of fighting my way back to a more normal level of functioning, at the age of forty-one, I was finally well enough to try golf. Why golf? Well, golf is a non-contact, low-impact sport, which was key due to the nature of my injuries.

I thought I should be able to hit a golf ball pretty easily, having played three sports in both high school and college. Haha—another false story my subconscious was telling me.

Anyone who's ever played golf has been quickly humbled. While it looks simple, it's actually very complicated to learn and understand. I wish I could say I struggled because I hadn't played sports for ten years, but that had nothing to do with it. As it turns out, hitting a ball that is just sitting there is a lot more difficult than it looks.

I often joke that golf is a lot like listening—it looks like you're doing nothing, but underneath the surface, you are working your ass off.

I decided it would be prudent to take some lessons after realizing I could not rely on any previous athletic experience to get better at golf. I marched myself down to the local golf course and signed up for eight private lessons with the golf pro. I thought, *This is great. I'll be on the path to becoming a better golfer before I know it.*

Unfortunately, my experience was very similar to countless golfers before me. Eight lessons later, I was no clearer about what I needed to do to consistently and effectively hit the golf ball. Why didn't lessons help me? I faithfully went to all eight, took notes, and practiced what the golf pro instructed. I went to the driving range on my own. I certainly didn't expect progress to come easily. I knew it would take practice and hard work to improve, which I willingly did. But I still ended up frustrated by my lack of progress.

One day I was talking about my frustration with my dad, who is an avid golfer. He told me a story about when he was in his twenties and working in Florida. At the time, he consistently scored in the seventies on the golf course, which is very good. My dad, also an avid learner, regularly took golf lessons while he was in Florida, and when he moved back to Pennsylvania, he decided to find a new golf pro.

Dad told me how upset he became after a few lessons with the new pro. The pro got him so confused that it totally screwed up his swing. It took him months to get it back on track. Dad said it was because the new pro made things so complicated and had him practicing the wrong things. Dad learned that the wrong help could be much worse than no help at all. He said, "I'll introduce you to the golf pro I work with now. He keeps things simple."

My dad and I lived almost two hours apart at the time, but while it was far less convenient, I decided to take his advice and schedule a lesson with the pro he recommended, Richard Garber. Richard's approach was very different from that of my previous golf pro. Richard kept things very simple. He basically had a system where you just needed to learn five things. All five work together to enable you to hit the ball consistently.

I'll digress here to share Richard's simple wisdom.

The five things you need to learn are:
1. The grip
2. How you set up in relation to the ball
3. How you take back the club
4. Hips start the back swing
5. Hips start the downswing

I began hitting the ball consistently after a few lessons using Richard's system and focusing on the five things. My score improved about twenty points in a year as I continued to practice. The reason I got results with Richard is he took something complex and hard to do and made it very simple. I got the results I wanted because I put in the time to practice and did not expect it to be easy.

Does needing to do only five things in a system sound familiar? It should. As we developed the Listening Path, I thought a lot about how Richard helped me understand golf and how to play the game. The simple system he created was the key to my success. Mastering a new skill is difficult; the simpler the process, the easier it is to learn. It takes time and effort to transform into something better.

WEEKEND VERSUS OLYMPIC ATHLETES

Speaking of simple versus easy, did you ever notice how effortlessly an expert makes their particular talent look? I have found when someone makes something look easy, it usually means they've put in hours and hours of hard work and effort. The ease with which experts practice a skill is disproportionate to the time and effort they put into making it look effortless.

The ease with which experts practice a skill is disproportionate to the time and effort they put into making it look effortless.

I'll often ask, "What is the difference between a weekend athlete and a professional or Olympic athlete?" The response I usually get is related to the number of hours of practice, Malcolm Gladwell's "10,000 hours." While the number of hours is a correct answer, the bigger insight is that the real difference is the speed and proficiency with which the athlete does the skill. For example, you can probably throw a football—so can Tom Brady. The fundamental difference is how well—accuracy, consistency, etc.—you each throw it. The number of hours spent practicing throwing a football is directly proportional to your speed and proficiency.

Let's review why transforming how you listen is so difficult. First, the subconscious is the enemy of listening well. This is at the root of people's struggle to be good at listening. Let's face it; not many of us are born with the natural athletic ability of listening, similar to how we are not born natural football stars.

The next problem is we have devoted education and training to telling and knowing instead of listening and understanding. Next, we have taught people to focus on attending to the listener. We expect the listener to know how to do complicated things such as empathize when they listen and ask the right questions without giving them the tools and showing them how. The final problem is overcoming the quick fix and instant change this fast-paced world desires and expects.

We've gotten you more than halfway to transforming how you listen. Understanding the Listening Path framework and tools is the simple part. The rest of the solution is in using the tools. If you want to improve your speed and proficiency as a listener, and transform from a weekend to an Olympic athlete, you need to use and practice the tools regularly.

The good news is you will have ample opportunity to practice these tools because you can apply them to any conversation— talking with the Uber driver, a customer service representative, the cashier at the dollar store, your spouse, your child, someone you say hello to on the street. You will find no shortage of opportunities to practice and apply these tools.

SUCCESS IS NOT AN ACCIDENT

Have you thought about when you've been successful and what you had to do to get there? We show a video in our workshops called *Stephen Curry: Success Is Not an Accident.* Alan Stein is the announcer and creator of the video. It's a great video and worth your time even if you aren't a sports or Stephen Curry fan.

On the video, Stein basically tells the story of how he was a coach at the first Kobe Bryant Nike Skills Academy where the top twenty high school and college players were invited to participate. Stein noted that while Stephen Curry was the least-known player, he was the most impressive because of his work ethic. Stein describes in detail all the intentional things Curry did to be successful—taking so many free throws before and after practice, showing up early, etc.—all with footage of many successful shots and moments, while people cheered in the stands.

The point of the video is we see the glory of Curry's success, the new beginning, when he became a successful NBA player. What we don't see is what happened before the success—we don't see the struggle of the story. We don't see that Curry's incredible work ethic and commitment to practice is what made him successful.

Stein says in the video, "Success is a choice," and asks out loud, "Are the habits you have today on par with the dreams you have for tomorrow? Further, whatever you do on a regular basis today will determine where you will be tomorrow."

I ask you, are your habits today on par with your dreams for tomorrow? What is your dream when it comes to transforming how you listen? Do you want to make a positive change in your life, work, or business? Do you want to improve your marriage, be a better parent, or drive more revenue to your business?

New Jersey mechanical contracting company Binksy and Snyder is one of our clients. The company has an amazing culture and core values that the CEO, Bob, and the HR head, Kelly, are committed to fostering and sustaining as the company grows. We have been working with the executive leadership team (ELT) on learning the Listening Path. Bob and Kelly understand that listening is at the core of solving problems and getting results.

Recently, one of the ELT members, Frank, said something I really appreciated. Frank said, "Every time I use the Listening Path and the tools, it works, and I have a positive result. Unfortunately, I'm not yet in the habit so I forget to use them when I get busy, and I go back to my old ways."

Frank is telling a story that a lot of people experience. There is no quick fix. Having the right tools to transform your listening only works if you use those tools. Success is not an accident.

ONE MOVE CHANGES YOUR GAME

Did you know that success starts with one move? Before we talk about, let me take you back. In Section Three, we covered all five Listening Path tools and included exercises to practice those tools in your everyday life. We've also focused on how the five tools work best when you use them together synchronously.

The approach to teaching in this book and in our workshops is designed to help you learn one move or tool at a time until you can put all five tools together, completely transforming how you listen.

I believe the best way to learn a new skill is to pick one thing you can apply and master it. After that one thing becomes second nature, master another. I learned the difference one skill or move can make when my high school field hockey coach, Linda, taught me something before starting my sophomore year in college.

We were watching Christy Morgan playing in a US field hockey game. Morgan was quite well known in the field hockey world, and watching her was like watching a famous Broadway performer. Morgan was dynamic, innovative, fierce, and at the top of her game. I was mesmerized as I watched her in action.

At one point, Morgan, a forward, broke away from the last defender and was in the scoring circle one-on-one against the goalie. I vividly remember Linda saying in that moment, "Watch this." It was as if everything went into slow motion as I watched intently.

What I expected to see next is what most people would have done, which is to take a hard shot on goal to beat the goalie. But that's not what happened. Instead, Morgan dribbled straight toward the goalie and, just before she was within reach, did a move called a "fake left, pull right." (Note: You can only use one side of the stick in field hockey.)

Morgan took her stick and faked left over the ball. The goalie followed the stick, opening the entire right side of the goal. Morgan then pulled the ball to her right, dribbling it into the goal. When I saw that, I said to myself, "I'm going to learn that move." I knew that move would help me overcome many of my athletic limitations.

I went home, put duct tape on my stick, and relentlessly dribbled in and out of cones in my driveway, faking left and pulling right.

I continued practicing for weeks until I had that one move mastered. That one move made a huge difference on the hockey field—and off. Mastering that one move not only helped me on the hockey field, but it led to coaching opportunities, which led to being recognized by influencers, and then more opportunities in my professional career. That one move had a ripple effect that lasted for years.

Did you know that success starts with one move?

DOING IT UNTIL....

Did you know that even the best moves don't work every time? Another principle about learning a new skill is that success isn't guaranteed. That was certainly the case with my fake left pull right move. While I was able to move past the defender most of the time, it didn't always work. Go figure—having a proven tool or move doesn't guarantee success every time. Who knew?

When I was working as a home-based therapist, we dealt with a lot of discipline issues between parents and children. I usually led the discussion by asking the parents what they had tried to curtail bad behavior. Parents usually said they'd tried everything—taking away the TV, the toys, grounding them, etc. Nothing worked. I felt as stuck as the parents did and, not knowing what to do next, asked for advice.

The clinicians training me said I was asking the wrong question. Instead of asking "What have you tried?", the better question was "What have you tried until it worked?" That question changed the game. Now, instead of trying everything they could think of, the parents focused on doing one thing until it worked. This made it much simpler and easy for them to hold their ground.

The same is true when applying the Listening Path tools. Do one thing until it works, because while it may not work every time, it will work most of the time.

KNOWING WHAT YOU ARE DOING

I want to mention one final thing about using and applying the tools. We frequently get the objection "What if the teller knows what I'm doing?" Remember the idea of affirming with the question "Do I get you?"? As a trained therapist, I felt sure that phrase was too in the teller's face and pushy about getting them to share their feelings. However, no one really noticed because it's such a powerful phrase.

Most of the time, people won't notice how you listen to them. However, no advantage comes from keeping the technique secret. Tell people you are using tools to be more effective. They will just appreciate that you are listening. We believe everyone should have a common language of listening.

In a perfect world, everyone in a company, a family, or a group of friends would use the five Listening Path tools. Everyone using the same tools to listen differently is a good idea all around. In fact, with a common language, you are more accountable for listening differently, and your skills improve.

I liken it to playing tennis. You must hit the ball back and forth. Your game improves when you play tennis with someone who is as good or better than you are. Conversely, your game regresses when you play someone who isn't as good. The same is true for listening. The better we are listened to, the better we are able to listen. A common listening language yields better results.

I have direct experience with this. Members of my team and people in my inner circle use the Listening Path tools with me and each other even when we're having a disagreement.

An example is when my boyfriend and I are at odds on an issue, and I feel angry or upset. When he says, "Tell me more," or "How does that make you feel?" I'll be honest, sometimes my internal reaction is, "How dare you use my own stuff on me!"

It's funny that, even though I have that conscious thought, I still want to answer, and I do, usually leading to me feeling less angry or frustrated and resolving the conflict.

EXERCISE

Have you honed in on practicing one skill? Which one have you been practicing, and what are the results?

_____

_____

_____

_____

CHAPTER SUMMARY

1. Story Gathering is simple by virtue of design. You will become a highly skilled story gatherer by synchronously using the five Listening Path tools and sticking with the process.

2. The simpler the process or framework, the easier it is to learn. While the framework is simple, transforming how you listen won't be easy. It requires practice and effort to transform into something better.

3. Having the right tools to transform your listening only works if you take them out and use them.

4. The level of ease with which the experts perform a skill is disproportionate to the time and effort they put into making it look effortless. It takes practice to make something look easy.

5. One move changes your game. Learn one move, or tool, at a time until you can combine the five tools, which will completely transform how you listen.

6. Success is not an accident; the habits you create today must align with the goals and dreams you have for tomorrow.

7. At EQuipt, we believe Story Gathering should be the common language for listening, where everyone uses the same path and tools to understand one another—profoundly changing how we interact and communicate.

?

- Chapter 19 -

EARNING THE RIGHT TO SOLVE AND SELL

"If you're not part of the solution, you're part of the problem."

— African Proverb

Success is not an accident. Most success can be attributed to the system, process, and/or tools you use. Systems and tools are not created equally and, therefore, can yield different results. Failure is inevitable if you spend time practicing the wrong thing. The Listening Path is simple by design, and we have given you proven tools to use individually, or ideally, together with family, friends, or coworkers to transform how you listen.

The question is: Are the habits you have today aligned with the dreams and goals you have for tomorrow?

While forming a new habit to apply the tools is not easy, the habit of using the tools will enable you to transform how you listen. We believe changing your game one move at a time is the quickest way to accomplish your goals. Practicing one move until it works will have a ripple effect of results.

Letting go of the worry that you are conspicuously using the tools to listen differently is also essential to success. Trust me; most people will not notice you are asking only six questions or affirming with "Do I get you?" They will just feel good that you are listening differently.

You now know that staying connected on the path while gathering the story from the teller and affirming a shared understanding transforms how you listen. It is time to learn how to change the conversation from understanding to helping solve the problem, guiding the teller to their tipping point, and finding the new beginning.

LISTENING HELPS SOLVE MOST PROBLEMS

Can listening solve all problems? Of course, not. Some problems cannot be solved. The loss of a loved one, terminal illness, a divorce, and the pain people have experienced can't be fixed/ changed. As the story gatherer, being unable to solve the problem can be uncomfortable because the desire is to help make things better.

The only solution is to give the gift of bearing witness or understanding the teller's pain. You may feel helpless or like you did not help enough, but bearing witness is a rare quality in a listener, colleague, friend, or even a stranger, and giving this gift is transformative in and of itself.

Did you know that listening is the precursor to solving problems?

I have had an interesting insight as I heightened my focus on what it costs not to listen. I've been in the business of listening my entire career, and it's taken me almost thirty years to boil it down to this: The more I focus on the problem of listening, the more I realize listening helps solve most problems.

People solve problems. The best ideas are exchanged when people communicate well, are aligned, focus on understanding rather than agreement, are connected, and trust one another. This creates the best solutions and the best outcomes. Too often we make more problems by prematurely trying to solve a problem without listening to understand first. When we first seek to understand, this understanding alone can be the solution.

When we first seek to understand, this understanding alone can be the solution.

A couple of years ago, I conducted a Listening Path workshop with about 100 attendees at a Women in Power (meaning electrical power) conference. I had just finished showing the "Breaktime with Michael Jr., Know Your Why" video I talked about in Chapter 4. As you recall, we get an overwhelmingly positive response to the video, and it is fun to watch the participants' reactions.

As I always do after the video, I asked the audience to tell me what they saw, noticed, observed. A woman raised her hand, stood up, and said the video was off-putting and even offensive to her. To be honest, I was quite surprised not only by her words, but by the veracity of her tone. I could see she was truly offended.

To give you a little more context, the woman was African-American and in her mid-thirties. Both the video host, Michael, and the singer, Darryl, were also African-American. To take you back to what happened in the video: Darryl sings "Amazing Grace" well the first time, but with little passion. Michael tells Darryl to sing it a particular way and then gives Darryl this backstory: "Your uncle just got out of jail, you got shot in the back when you were a kid, I'm just saying, show me the hood version." The audience in the video and my audience laughed simultaneously. Then Darryl proceeded to sing a second time with tremendous passion and purpose.

The woman in my audience said she did not like the negative and racial stereotypes in the backstory given by the host. In that moment, I was completely mortified. I immediately felt defensive since the last thing I wanted to do was offend anyone or be thought of as insensitive to racial concerns and biases. I was also thinking we had shown the video throughout the world to all ethnic and racial groups and gotten an overwhelmingly positive response with no pushback.

Then, my defense attorney came raging in from my subconscious! I thought, *How dare she say this to me in front of this room full of people?*

Just as I was about to plead my case, tell her why she was wrong, and defend myself, I paused. I decided to take a different approach. I decided to find out where she was coming from.

I asked her to please tell me more. She did, talking about the backstory the comedian gave the singer and her perception of it.

While I still felt defensive, I realized I had no right to try to talk this woman out of her feelings because I am not African-American and do not know what it is like living as a minority. I also thought I should hear her out to see if we needed to rethink showing the video in the future. I continued on the Listening Path, and after she finished talking, I said, "Let me see if I get you...." Then I followed up by reflecting her story in about thirty seconds.

Truthfully, I was already trying to figure out how we could find another video that made the point about *what versus why* and how to be a great, inspirational singer for our workshops. I knew that was going to be tough to find.

What happened next really surprised me. After I reflected the woman's feelings and story, she took a deep breath and totally changed her tone and perspective. She went on to say that, in hindsight, she had overreacted to that part of the video and saw how truly inspirational it was, how it made the point about singing to the right story. She said she felt better, thanked me, and sat down.

I didn't have to do anything to solve the problem, hers or mine. I had stepped back, asked her to tell me more, and reflected her story. By taking the approach of understanding to appreciate her perspective, her feelings, and see her, she pivoted, solving the problem for us both.

Understanding is a very important aspect of problem-solving. While sometimes the problem still needs solving, understanding alone can also solve the problem itself.

EXERCISE

Have you experienced having to step back and listen to the teller, even when your defense attorney wanted to kick in?

_____

_____

_____

_____

EARNING THE RIGHT

When do you know you've earned the right to change the conversation? What does earning the right mean? The well-known sales methodology and book *The Challenger Sale* by Matthew Dixon and Brent Adamson describes the idea. The gist of the book is that it takes more than being a relationship builder to sell successfully. The contention is relationship selling may work when you are selling something simple, like a car, but Dixon and Adamson maintain that in complex business to business sales, the successful seller is the one who plays the challenger. The salesperson who teaches, tailors, and controls the conversation with the customer wins.

This teaching, tailoring, and controlling wins the business and provides the correct solution in a complex sale. I emphatically agree with this premise. It is fundamental to being a consultant to your customers and for them to learn from you. As the seller, you should drive value by guiding your customers to a better solution, creating success for both you and them. The relationship alone is not enough.

Here is what I also believe: To teach, tailor, and control the customer conversation, you first must earn their trust and confidence and deeply understand them and their business problems.

Remember, people do not like to be told, taught, and certainly not controlled. Without setting the foundation of trust and truly understanding both the customer and their business, you will either get grin-fucked or thrown out on your ass.

About six years ago, my friend Marv Perel, whom I introduced you to earlier, and I went out to a small company that designed custom products. Dupont manufactured materials this company needed, so the Dupont sales reps would call on them frequently. Since Dupont was the first adopter of the Challenger Sale Methodology, Marv was very curious about the small company's experience working with the Dupont sales reps.

During my initial presentation, Marv was in the back of the room asking the attendees to tell him more and using the other six Listening Path questions to learn more about their experience with Dupont.

When Marv and I walked out to the parking lot together, he said, "I asked them what the Dupont sales reps were like." They had told Marv, "Well, Dupont is the biggest player in the market, and their salespeople used to be kind of arrogant. In recent years, after they went through Challenger Sales Training, they are just obnoxious, acting as if they know more about our business than we do."

This story affirmed what Marv and I already knew. Sure, you need to teach people, tailor, and control the sale, but unless you earn the right to do so first, the approach of teaching, telling, and controlling the customer is obnoxious. First, you must take the time to gather the story and confirm you understand both the person and their situation. Then, and only then, have you earned the right to change the conversation to one in which you solve the problem or show them a solution.

YOU ARE THE TIPPING POINT

How do you know you have earned the right to change the conversation and provide the answer or solution? It is pretty simple if you picture the path, the map, and the four stops. In most conversations about a current struggle, the teller has not yet hit a tipping point and certainly has not gotten to the new beginning. You, as the story gatherer, want to gather the story's beginning and struggle. Once you have gathered the whole story, mini-reflected, and reflected in thirty to ninety seconds to affirm you got them, guide the teller to the tipping point. The tipping point is you and how you can help them solve the problem.

From a business perspective, you may be helping with an employee's concern, making recommendations on a project, providing a technology solution, or recommending services or products. On the personal side, you may be talking to your spouse, who is struggling with a problem, or with a friend, parent, or child, and is unsure how to

The tipping point is you and how you can help them solve the problem.

handle the situation. When you gather well and truly understand, you have earned the right to tell, advise, collaborate, sell, and/or solve.

When I started my executive coaching and training company in 2007, I landed one of my biggest clients on my very first call. I sat down with Tony, the CEO of a public orthobiologics company. Tony was only thirty-six when he took over the company as CEO. The company was nearly bankrupt then, but Tony had raised significant venture capital over five years to revive the company. Tony said he had a new, more sophisticated board of directors who had high expectations of his highly qualified but rather young leadership team.

After this short background story, Tony handed me a brochure from another training company, and said, "I need training for my leadership team." On one hand, this was music to my ears. Leadership training was one of my core offerings, and I had done a lot of it over the years. On the other hand, I had no idea what kind of training Tony thought his leadership team needed.

I almost took the sales bait and gave Tony what he was asking for: a solution. I sat there thinking I didn't have a pretty brochure like the other company, nor did I genuinely know what training his team needed.

I kept asking Tony to take me back and tell me more. I didn't realize it at the time, but because I didn't have the answer, I was forced to stay in the beginning and the struggle of his story. I remember Tony asking me just to give him a proposal like the other company had done while holding up their glitzy brochure and folder.

I challenged him, asking, "Did they specifically put this together for you or is this cookie cutter?"

Tony laughed, and said, "Probably the latter."

Tony then began to slow down and, instead of rushing, wanting me just to give him a solution; we talked about the problem itself, getting to the heart of the issue. Evidently, the team went into the first board meeting with a 120 slide PowerPoint presentation. The board scolded Tony, questioning how his team was qualified to understand their market if they did not know how to under-stand and present to the board. I was then clear—not only on the problem, but on what Tony's people needed and how I could help.

CREATING THE NEW BEGINNING

By listening differently and not rushing to solve the problem, Tony and I began to build the new beginning of his story. Initially, Tony thought his team needed training on presentation skills. I helped him see that coaching his team on how to understand and man-age the board was a better place to start.

During our meeting, Tony didn't ask for help for himself, only for his team. Ultimately, Tony came to his own insight—it is part of what makes him such an incredible CEO and leader. As we were setting up, he turned to me and said, "I think I should go first. You need to coach me too."

Tony and I worked together for four years until the company was sold. The first meeting with Tony, like one move, had a ripple effect. That initial engagement with Tony's senior team led to business for me working with hundreds of people because we established a coaching arm to develop his employees company-wide.

Do you see how listening earns you the right to solve? Do you see how you are the tipping point in the story?

EXERCISE

Describe an instance when you were the tipping point in the story. Explain how the conversation went.

_____

_____

_____

_____

CHAPTER SUMMARY

1. Listening is the precursor to solving problems. The best ideas are exchanged when people communicate well, are aligned, focus on understanding rather than agreement, are connected, and trust one another.

2. We often create more problems by prematurely trying to solve a problem without listening to understand first.

3. When we first seek to understand, the resulting understanding alone can be the solution.

4. The key to solving problems effectively is staying in the beginning and the struggle of the teller's story until you truly understand the problem.

5. As the story gatherer, you want to completely gather the story's beginning and struggle. Once you have gathered, mini-reflected, reflected in thirty to ninety seconds, and affirmed that "you got them," you then become the tipping point in the teller's story.

6. By taking the time to understand the teller's story, you earn the right to solve the problem.

7. When you gather well and truly understand, you have also earned the right to create the new beginning of the teller's story...the right to tell, advise, collaborate, sell, and solve.

?

Chapter 20

LISTENING'S IMPORTANCE

"Most successful people I've known are the ones who do more listening than talking."

— Bernard M. Baruch

The more I focus on solving the problem of listening, the more I come to realize that listening helps solve most problems. Sometimes the teller will come to the solution on their own just by virtue of you gathering their story, reflecting, and understanding. Other times, gathering earns you the right to be the tipping point in the teller's story, which opens the door to them allowing you to help shape their new beginning.

Too often, people rush to solve the problem prematurely, and sometimes the one who is rushing to solve the problem is the teller.

Too often, people rush to solve the problem prematurely, and sometimes the one who is rushing to solve the problem is the teller. Either way, as the story gatherer, you are there to be the guide on the path, slow both of you down, and follow the same footsteps on the path. The key to solving problems effectively is staying in the beginning and the struggle until you truly understand the problem. While this is just common sense in theory, in practice, it is more difficult than it looks.

Listening is recognized as one of the most important business skills for a reason. Simply put, listening, or not listening, affects every part of an organization and/or relationship. Have you considered how much power listening has and why? As we have discussed throughout this book, we are not used to thinking about how listening affects outcomes.

Why is listening so powerful? First, I'll start with how listening helps breathe life into an organization. Next, we'll look at the power of listening in ten specific areas; these are just some of the ways listening makes a difference.

LISTENING IS OXYGEN

Why is listening so powerful? Organizations and relationships are systems, just like humans. Listening is like oxygen in the system that helps sustain life. When a human suffers from heart disease, slowly but surely the organs start to die due to the restriction of oxygen flowing through the system. This restricted blood flow happens gradually and in such a way that is not noticeable, until it is.

About twenty years ago, my ex-father-in-law ended up in the hospital on the brink of having a massive heart attack. My sister-in-law, who worked in the heart catheter lab of the local hospital, was visiting my father-in-law when she noticed something was wrong. Her experience and fast action ultimately saved his life. She got him in an ambulance and directly to the catheter lab, bypassing (seriously, no pun intended here) the emergency department. When my ex, Michael, and I got to my father-in-law's room where he was waiting to be taken into surgery, I remember looking at Michael and saying, "Wow, Dad looks amazing." I was expecting to see a man close to death, but what I saw was a man who looked more alive than he had in years.

Apparently, my father-in-law's oxygen levels were so low when he arrived at the hospital that just by virtue of them pumping oxygen through his system, he was already looking and feeling better. This, of course, was a temporary fix.

My father-in-law had four stents implanted to open the blockages, creating a longer-term solution that got the blood and oxygen flowing. Fortunately, my father-in-law lived many more healthy years, passing away at eighty-eight.

In organizations and relationships, listening and understanding are the oxygen that needs to flow throughout the entire system to breath in good health and a higher quality of life.

Without understanding, people feel tired, frustrated, and like they do not matter. In time, they may leave. According to Gallup's *State* of *the American Manager* report in 2017, "One in two employees have left a job to get away from a manager."

Let's go back to what makes the great ones great. It's managers and leaders who make people feel good. They get the best out of their people and retain them.

Listening differently has profound benefits when it comes to making people feel valued and thus increasing job satisfaction—and life satisfaction, for that matter. Have you considered how important listening well is to you and your employees, to your organization? Are you pumping oxygen into your organization by listening and understanding? Let's take a look at some of the areas in which listening makes all the difference.

MAKING DECISIONS AND LEADERSHIP

How much of your day is spent listening? Reminder, estimates indicate managers and employees spend at least 40 percent of their time listening, while executives spend up to 80 percent of their workdays listening to assess information, gain new insights, and make changes. As leaders, listening is key, not only in our ability to make decisions, but more importantly, for the quality of those decisions.

Decision-making can be defined as the process of selecting a right and effective course of action from two or more alternatives for the purpose of achieving a desired result. Decision-making is the essence of management. According to Dalton E. McFarland in his book *Management: Principles and Practices*, "Decision are a choice, wherein an executive forms a conclusion about what must be done in a given situation. A decision represents a behavior chosen from several alternatives."

Have you ever made a choice where you were choosing between three alternatives? If you had thirty alternatives instead, would that be significantly harder?

I am probably dating myself again here, but when I was growing up and needed a pair of sneakers, we had relatively few options compared to today. Deciding which pair of sneakers to buy was a much easier choice back then. Today, when I need a pair of sneakers, I go on Zappos, use the filter to narrow my choices based on exactly what I am looking for—size, color, etc.—and I still have thirty or more options to choose from.

Buying shoes takes a lot longer than if I only had a few choices. However, the quality of my decision is much better, as I end up with sneakers that are far better suited to me.

Listening well, gathering the full story, informs a leader's decision-making in a couple of ways. One, when you really listen, you uncover a lot of information, which is necessary to making good decisions. If you don't listen well, you limit the information you are basing your decision on.

Two, as a leader, you rely on people for information to help you make informed decisions. Your decision's quality is based to a great extent on your ability to listen to your people and discover the real story and, ultimately, the insights within the data others have collected.

EXERCISE

Think of a time when you didn't listen well and then made a poor decision.

_____

_____

EMPOWERING EMPLOYEES AND TEAMS

How does listening help empower our employees and teams? We've all heard the proverb, "Give someone a fish, and you feed them for a day. Teach them to fish and you feed them for a lifetime." The *Oxford English Dictionary* defines empowerment as, "authority or power given to someone to do something. The process of becoming stronger and more confident."

Empowerment is one of the trickier aspects of managing and leading people. Truly giving them the authority and building their confidence, especially when it is beyond the scope of their experience, is difficult. People are generally not skilled at truly knowing how to empower their employees and teams because we are taught to talk and tell. The subconscious says, "I told them what to do, so now they can go do it." This is giving them a fish.

True empowerment is to teach them to fish so they can eat for a lifetime. The ability to coach and teach is a core competency for an effective leader and/or manager. Most managers and leaders are not taught how to be coaches. It is more often an assumed skill. While we throw a little bit of training at it, most of the training is on the job, where we learn by trial and error.

An effective coach has two key qualities. First, they must believe in people's competence. It is difficult to coach and empower if they don't believe people are competent at their core. The second quality is the ability to ask the right questions rather than giving the coachee, or the employee, the answers.

Once again, we can ask a lot of questions as a coach, but that doesn't mean we are asking the right questions. The defense attorney shows up in all kinds of conversations.

Here's where listening comes in. When you use the Listening Path tools, you help your team tell their story, and as the coach, you gather it. As you guide them along the path, once they have shared their beginning and struggle, they start to gain a greater understanding of their story just by you gathering it.

Going back to the beginning is one of the best things you can ask them to do when empowering and coaching. It's also a best practice to teach employees to ask themselves to do so. Once you gather the beginning and struggle, and confirm everyone feels understood, "Do we get each other?", you enable and empower them. Rather than giving them the answer, you become the tipping point by having them think about how best to navigate to the new beginning.

You can have your team do this in the moment or have them work together to come up with what they think are the best solutions. You will be there merely as a sounding board to listen and reflect.

Story Gathering is a key component in empowering your teams as you shift from telling them what to do to helping them uncover the best answers. With this approach, your team will develop more innovative approaches to solving problems.

RESOLVING CONFLICT

What is your perception of conflict? Is it positive or negative? Do you see conflict as an opportunity to make improvements in your relationships at work or at home? Many of us find conflict unpleasant, and therefore, avoid it at all costs.

We do an exercise with our clients about their perceptions of and feelings about conflict. We ask them to write down five words they associate with conflict and then assign a positive, negative, or neutral meaning to each word. Even the rating of positive, negative, or neutral is subjective. For example, one word might be discord—for some that word is negative, others see it as positive, still others see it as neutral. After we have them assign meaning to each word, we have them calculate the percentage of positive and negative on a scale of 0 to 100 percent.

Then we have the team stand in the back of the room on an imaginary continuum of 0 to 100 percent, showing them where they are in relation to each other on the conflict percentage scale. It's fascinating to see where people end up and their reactions. Very quickly, they can see how the person who sees conflict as 100 percent positive relates to the person who sees conflict as 100 percent negative.

It's also surprising to people how many dominant personality styles are on the side of perceiving conflict as negative. Being assertive or direct is not the same as believing conflict is positive.

How does listening and gathering the story help us manage conflict differently? It is extremely important to note that understanding has nothing to do with agreement. Just because I understand how you feel and see something doesn't mean I have to agree with it. I really hate the idea of "Let's just agree to disagree." I believe this is as overused as "I understand." Instead of "Let's agree

It is extremely important to note that understanding has nothing to do with agreement.

to disagree," how about we shift to "I agree to understand"? At least we leave the conversation and our relationship at "I understand you," rather than "I disagree with you."

One reason conflict is perceived negatively is it can be very difficult to resolve, especially when we are far apart on an issue, and a compromise, or win-win, is unlikely. People struggle with resolving conflict because they start by focusing on what they disagree about, rather than what they agree on. You may be totally misaligned and disagree on the fundamental issue at hand, but you can start resolving the conflict simply by understanding first.

Gather the story you are seeking to understand. That leads to the first area of agreement, "I understand you and you understand me." When we understand one another, the issue itself becomes easier to resolve.

GETTING THINGS DONE

Have you ever thought about how important listening is to getting things done? At EQuipt, we work a lot with teams who are stuck and struggling to work together to get things done.

A few years ago, we worked with a leadership team at a global company that specializes in the best practices for project management training. The team of eight was struggling to get things done when the CEO wasn't in the room. When the CEO was there, he would intervene by making the decision for the team because they weren't able to come to the decision themselves. When he wasn't there, everything stalled, and people focused on their individual goals versus what was best for the larger team and business.

When they asked for a proposal describing how we could help, we talked about our approach of learning to present yourself with passion and purpose and transforming how you listen as the starting point. I like to refer to it as the foundation of the house.

This team was frustrated individually and collectively, highly impatient, and wanted to get on with making some critical decisions. When we opened the session with discussing what makes the great ones great, they looked like their heads were going to explode. They did not see how presenting yourself properly and learning to listen differently was part of the solution for helping them solve problems together.

A common problem we face when teams are stuck is they don't see the relevance of our process to their situation. They want to dive right into the issues, rather than slowing down to speed up.

When we start by slowing them down, they can resist and become easily frustrated. We've learned not to take this struggle personally. Instead, we empathize, understand, and become the helpful guide to get them to the tipping point.

We got to the point in the first session where we sent the team into breakout sessions to practice the Listening Path tools by sharing a "best failure story," a story about a mistake they each made and learned something great from.

When we sent them into the breakout rooms, the human resources head, who was an advocate and the one who hired us, felt the team's tension, and said, "Christine, I don't think we have time for this. We have got to get to some of the critical decisions we as a team need to make."

Feeling her pain and anxiety, I said, "I imagine you're really worried that we won't get some critical problems solved. Please trust me. You'll see why this makes sense in about an hour."

The team went into the breakout groups tense, surly, frustrated, and doubtful. An hour and a half later, when they walked back into the conference room, they were laughing, smiling, and looking more relaxed and connected.

When we debriefed the Listening Path practice exercise, the feedback included, "I learned a lot about my teammates," and "Now I understand why they approach things this way or that way."

In addition to learning how to slow down and really listen to each other, the team also learned a little more about what makes each other tick.

We were able to discuss the difficult problems more effectively because we started by having the team get to know and understand each other. The team was more open and receptive to hearing conflicting opinions and being better at listening to understand and gain insights. This was the beginning of helping them change their culture to get things done together—without the CEO's intervention.

LISTENING MAKES YOU SMARTER

Did you know that listening makes you smarter? You might be

thinking, *Well, of course, it does.* When you listen well, you uncover information, have insights, and learn things that make you more intelligent in so many ways, from what you know to how you enhance your emotional quotient. However, here's my favorite part of how listening makes you smarter.

When you really gather the story, while people often come to their own answers, they give you the credit for giving them the answer. Let me tell you what I mean.

One of our clients is Germantown Academy (GA), a well-known private school in the Philadelphia area. I met my good friend Sue when she was an undergrad student on the field hockey team when I was in grad school. Twenty-plus years later, she is the head of the grade school at GA. Sue is an incredible leader— innovative, connected, gets things done, strategic, and she fervently listens to the entire school community, including her team and the parents. Sue will occasionally request a coaching session to go over what she's working on and ensure she's not missing anything.

About eighteen months ago, Sue and I met in her office. As usual, Sue came prepared with a list of things she wanted to process, talk through, and figure out. I did what I usually do—that is, I gathered, said take me back, tell me more, reflected, asked if I got her, etc.

After about ninety minutes, Sue looked at me, sat back in her chair, and said, "Christine, I always find it so helpful to meet with you. You always give me such good advice and answers. I feel so much better."

In that moment, I felt like such a fraud. Up to that point, the only thing I had done was reflect the answers Sue already had and help her narrow them down so she could decide the best course.

I had a decision to make—tell Sue, both my client and friend, what was really going on, or let her keep believing the story she was telling herself, the story where I was the one with the answers.

I decided to fess up. I said, "Sue, I really appreciate that I was helpful to you, but the truth is, I didn't have the answers. You did. I just helped you see them."

As Sue thought about our conversation, she saw that was exactly what had happened. Then we both laughed.

I have never felt like the smartest person in the room based on my deficiencies in many subject areas, including math and science to name just a couple. However, I've received a lot of credit for being really smart when the truth is I have simply listened well to the really smart people as they found the answers within.

DIVERSITY, EQUITY, AND INCLUSION (DEI)

Listening to understand is the beginning of closing the gap between our experiences based on the unique aspects of our primary and secondary dimensions. Primary dimensions are the things that individuals typically cannot alter. Secondary dimensions are acquired or changed by our environment. Even if we don't agree, understanding these different dimensions and getting beyond them closes the gap and gets us one step closer to working together to solve problems.

In 2020, we saw tremendous unrest over racial inequities. The pandemic disproportionately affected African-Americans and video of black people being injured and killed by police shined a spotlight on these issues and increased the debate and awareness of the issue of diversity, equity, and inclusion (DEI). As a species, we have made significant progress on this problem over the years, but unfortunately, it persists in organizations and the world in general. We have a very long way to go.

I certainly don't profess to have all the answers on the subject or know how to solve all the problems, but I do believe transforming how people listen would be a major step forward.

Recently, I read the article "Elevating Equity: The Real Story of Diversity and Inclusion" by Josh Bersin. In it, he reported on a study that surveyed more than 800 organizations, analyzed more than eighty different practices, and correlated them against a variety of outcomes to determine which practices matter most. They concluded that there are five essential strategies for DEI excellence. Guess what was named number one—listen, hear, act.

Like resolving any conflict or working through differing perspectives, weeding through the complex layers of diversity, equity, and inclusion requires a healthy, open, and trusting dialogue. Having difficult conversations is part of creating a better way and solving the difficult problems we face.

In my experience, most people don't know how to have these very difficult conversations about our differences, especially in the political climate we live in. For example, when asking what is it like to be African-American, be transgender, or have a child who is gay, people fear they will say the wrong thing, leading them to saying nothing at all.

We have come to the point where we don't know what is and what is not okay to say, so we aren't having any meaningful conversations. On top of this, we are all biased. The stories that reside in our subconscious are not always something we are proud of, and, in fact, can be a source of shame.

It is difficult to admit to ourselves, let alone others, our biases, thoughts, and feelings. Learning to story gather sets the tone for wanting to understand ourselves, others, their experiences, and walking in their shoes.

When we all come from a perspective of, "I want to understand what it's like for you, to be in your shoes," we can get down to the business of finding a better way to be accepting and inclusive of all.

EXERCISE

List three ways you can become more inclusive by listening.

_____

_____

_____

EMPLOYEE ENGAGEMENT

Did you know, according to *Forbes*, "Seventy-seven percent of employees say they'd work longer hours for an empathetic employer. Ninety-five percent of employees are motivated to work longer or harder for an employer who is empathetic toward them"?

In May 2020, Gallup came out with their latest statistic on employee engagement. They found that 49 percent of workers are not engaged and are psychologically detached from their work. What I found both astonishing and depressing is that this engagement statistic was at an all-time high.

Somehow, a statistic that shows slightly more than half of the employee base is actually engaged is a reason to celebrate.

Like diversity, equity, and inclusion, I don't profess to have all the answers, but what I do know is employee engagement is better when employers listen to their employees.

In December 2020, our client Binsky and Snyder wanted to develop a plan to bring the workers safely back to the office after working remotely during the pandemic. Many employers sent out a survey to employees requesting feedback on how they would like the reintegration to happen and the future model of the workplace.

The Binsky team decided to go the extra mile to ensure the team felt heard and understood. Together, we developed a "connection team," a team that would learn the Listening Path framework and tools so they could listen to understand. Next, each member of the team set up a virtual meeting to listen to three members of the organization who did not report to or work with them directly. We used the six questions, specific questions we developed, and "Do I get you?" as the platform for getting feedback.

I participated in the first interviews with connection team members so I could give them feedback on how they listened and used the Listening Path tools. The feedback we received included, "It means a lot to me that leadership wants to hear and listen to employees," and "Taking the time to get my opinion and hear my thoughts really means a lot."

When you take the time to ask, listen, gather, and understand, employees feel important, recognized, and more engaged. They become part of the solution and the team.

SELLING

According to Web Strategies, "Ninety-five percent of buyers state that the typical salesperson talks too much." This hurts sales. The solution is simple—listen differently. Listen, understand, and uncover insights, and see what happens.

IMPROVING YOURSELF

How does listening help me improve myself? In 2013, the business world was focused on storytelling. Despite this, I decided to swim against the storytelling tidal wave and focus on Story Gathering because I strongly believed that gathering was the precursor to telling and the more vital skill. Here is why.

If we don't know the story going on in another's subconscious, we won't know which story to tell to help people overcome their reluctance to change. Gathering and discovering the story first helps us know the right story to tell, one that paints a picture that will inspire teams to change and see the new beginning.

I mentioned in Chapter 4 that, fundamentally, self-awareness is understanding your moods and your thoughts about your moods. In neuroscience terms, what story are you telling yourself in your subconscious? Gathering your own story and discovering the story you are telling yourself inherently raises your EQ and/or self-awareness.

As you raise self-awareness, you also increase your ability to regulate yourself in difficult situations and navigate through those difficulties with more calm and resilience. These are just some of the things that EQ does for us. However, if we don't practice listening to ourselves first and understanding our own story, we miss a huge opportunity to give ourselves the gift we can ultimately give others—finding the hidden gems and insights.

IMPROVING RELATIONSHIPS

Do you want to be a better listener at home? On this journey together of learning how to listen in a transformative way, I have shared the importance of listening differently on both business and personal relationships.

I would be remiss if I didn't take a moment to step back and emphasize that learning to be a better listener to someone you love will have a profoundly beautiful effect on your relationship. It is truly the oxygen that helps nourish and sustain your relationship.

It seems that when we are with someone for a long time, like being married for twenty years, we come to believe we should know our partner well enough to know what they are thinking. That, of course, is a listening inhibitor—the mind reading thing.

The truth is, no matter how well we know someone, it is impossible to read their mind. Taking it for granted that we know someone is also a way to constrict the arteries that supply oxygen. People change and grow over time. Our relationships stagnate if we don't walk in the same footsteps on the path together or we disconnect because we are not checking in.

When I started my career as a therapist, I had a hard time understanding why couples divorced after twenty-plus years. What I heard repeatedly in couples counseling was that when the kids came along, everything started to be about them. Couples lost focus and stopped nurturing their relationship. They no longer had anything in common. When the children were grown and out of the house, they were strangers.

Life is busy, with lots of demands from work, kids, parents, finances, etc., and it's difficult to prioritize listening to understand our partner. A lot of noise and static can develop between two people, and they can end up on different frequencies. People who have embraced the Listening Path and used the tools have said they can feel the person they love more because they hear what they are not saying. It's as if they have been able to reduce the static and get on the same frequency. Doing so not only maintains but strengthens the foundation of any relationship.

Are you on the same frequency with your life partner, your children, your employees? Listening is the way we ensure we are on the same path and frequency. Relationships, whether business or personal, are about helping the other person feel appreciated, understood, and ultimately, loved.

EXERCISE

How can you improve your personal and work relationships by using the Listening Path tools?

_____

_____

_____

_____

CHAPTER SUMMARY

1. Listening is like oxygen, breathing life into organizations and relationships.

2. Without understanding, people feel tired, frustrated, and insignificant.

3. Executives and managers spend 40 to 80 percent of their time listening to make decisions and uncover insights. Decision quality reduces as you listen less.

4. Story Gathering is a key component in empowering teams as you shift from telling them what to do to helping them uncover the best answers.

5. Understanding does not imply agreement. I can understand your feelings and point of view without agreeing with them.

6. People struggle with resolving conflict because they often start by focusing on what they disagree about, rather than where they agree. Understanding first creates alignment and opportunity for conflict resolution.

7. Listening makes you smarter. When you gather the story, people often come to their own answers, and they give you the credit.

8. Primary dimensions of diversity are the things that individuals typically cannot alter, while secondary dimensions are acquired or changed over time. Seeking to understand closes the gap and gets us one step closer to working together to solve differences.

9. The bottom line is that listening is good for the bottom line. Listening well positively touches every aspect of an organization by deepening connections and trust. When connection is abundant, we solve problems better, get things done, have difficult conversations, empower others, manage conflict, and help employees feel and stay engaged.

?

- Chapter 21 -

STORY SELLING, THE OTHER SIDE OF GATHERING

"Storytelling offers the opportunity to talk with your audience, not at them."

— Laura Holloway

Organizations and relationships are living systems that need oxygen to breath and thrive. When we listen well, gathering the story to really understand, we have an abundant supply of oxygen. When we listen poorly, telling and talking, we restrict the oxygen supply to the system, slowly killing it. Listening well positively touches every aspect of an organization by deepening connections and trust. When connection is abundant, we solve problems more effectively, get things done, have difficult conversations, empower others, manage conflict, and help employees feel and stay engaged. The bottom line is listening is good for the bottom line.

The bottom line is listening is good for the bottom line.

You've done it—you have the tools

you need to transform how you listen to understand! You know how to earn the right to tell someone what to do. However, telling is still not the most effective way to create action.

While listening is the most powerful form of communication, a story is the best way to tell someone something. Even when you've earned the right, telling will more likely cause resistance than telling a story. The story reaches the emotional, limbic brain that resides in the subconscious. The emotional brain is where people decide to act. Once you have gathered the beginning and the struggle of the story, understanding the person and their problems, you've earned the right to help them solve them. This is where you shift from Story Gathering to storytelling. You become the tipping point, and rather than telling someone what to do, you share a story that shows them how to get to their new beginning. We call this story selling; the story will do the telling and selling for you.

STORYTELLING, ANOTHER UNDERDEVELOPED SKILL

Did you know that people retain 65-70 percent of information shared through stories and only 5-10 percent through a dry presentation of data and statistics? This is according to the London School of Business. Even if you have earned the right to tell someone what to do, you have to make people want to listen. Too commonly, people approach the telling part of communication by providing logical arguments or data.

In business, we use glitzy PowerPoint presentations with charts and graphs to try to impress and convince. Logic, data, and pretty PowerPoints are not what make people want to listen.

The answer to this problem is to tell a story that includes both facts and feelings. While this is widely understood, storytelling remains a skill that is grossly underdeveloped and underused. Like listening, telling a story is harder than it looks.

USING THE SAME PATH

Do you consider yourself a good storyteller? We ask a lot of our clients and workshop participants this question. Our experience is that only about a quarter of people think they are decent or good storytellers. Estimates indicate storytelling has been around for anywhere from 36,000 to 95,000 years. We have used stories to pass down information about religion, medicine, traditions, etc. since the days when the cave dwellers used pigment to create stories on the walls.

If it's been around so long, why is storytelling such a difficult skill to build?

Here's what's interesting. The human brain is wired to want to hear, learn, and be told through stories. However, our brains are not wired to be natural storytellers. The latter of the two, the knowing how to effectively tell a story, is a skill, like listening, that must be learned. Another advantage of learning how to gather a story before you build or tell one is that when you learn the path to gathering a story, you are also learning the path to telling a story.

In Chapter 15, I said during the thirty to ninety seconds reflection, you temporarily switch from being the story gatherer to being the storyteller as you reflect the teller's story back to them. All along the path of how to be a story gatherer, you've been learning and practicing being a storyteller, and you didn't even know it.

We created the Listening Path with the idea that the path you need to gather a story is the exact same path to building and telling a story. Story Gathering and storytelling are inextricably linked—the path to success is the same for both.

TELLING A STORY IN BUSINESS

Do you tell stories in your personal life but not at work? I know the answer is yes. Think about it. It's holiday time or you have a reunion with a group of friends you haven't seen forever. What do you do? You tell stories about what happened years ago when you were in high school, college, or just hanging out. With your family, you share memories of when Dad tried to fry the turkey and burned it to a crisp, or your brother broke his arm doing something stupid. These are all stories. They are just in the form of memories.

The difference between telling a story in our personal lives and in a business setting is that in our personal lives, our stories don't necessarily have to have a point. In business they do. This is part of what makes telling a story in business so hard and why Story Gathering is the precursor of telling.

First, I need to know what story my audience, my customer, my employee, is telling themselves, or at least try to imagine what the story could be. Then I need to figure out the point of my story and make sure that point is directly in line with what my audience needs to hear to overcome the story they are telling themselves.

Discovering and relating what's in it for the listener is the key to storytelling in business.

EXERCISE

Think of the last time you told a story in business. Map out the path of that story:

Beginning:

_____

_____

_____

Struggle:

_____

_____

_____

Tipping point:

_____

_____

_____

New beginning:

_____

_____

_____

LET THE STORIES DO THE SELLING

Recently, I met with Kelly, a woman I work closely with at one of the companies we serve. She is in her mid-thirties, a manager and leader, and recognized for having a lot of potential. Kelly was about to go out on maternity leave for three months and was asking for help to ensure her team was ready to handle things without her.

Kelly was concerned they would not have the confidence that they could handle things in her absence. Kelly was especially worried about a very competent and respected team member who tended to say she was overwhelmed when there was a lot going on. Overwhelmed didn't mean she couldn't handle it; she just was the type to express it out loud. Kelly wanted to make sure her team member was aware of who was around before she expressed her feelings. Kelly wasn't sure how to help this employee understand the effect on perception her saying she was overwhelmed could have.

After Kelly shared the background, I told her a story about a time when I was in high school during hockey pre-season. I was starting my senior year as one of the team captains.

After a practice game, I was sitting on the bench with my best friend Sue, laughing and goofing around while watching a junior varsity game. Linda, our coach, was in front of us talking with the person who officiated our varsity game. As Sue and I were goofing around, I got animated and loudly said the word *shit*. Both Linda and the official heard me, and Linda turned to me and said, "Go run a lap." I immediately took off. Clearly, shit was not the worst word I ever said, but I was mortified because I could see I had disappointed Linda, whom I respected and adored.

I felt terrible that I had crossed a line and embarrassed her in front of the official. Then something happened that really surprised me. About fifteen minutes later, Linda came over to me privately and said, "Christine, I really don't care if you say shit, but please be aware of your surroundings. If you swear in front of the official, you don't give me a choice. I have to make you run."

After I finished my story, Kelly and I continued our conversation. Within about two minutes, Kelly looked at me and said, "Two things. How do you remember things that happened twenty years ago?" (Inside, I laughed because it was a lot longer than twenty years ago.) Then Kelly said, "Second, that was a really helpful story."

Rather than my telling Kelly what to do, we started to figure out a story she could tell her team member to make the point. Stories are much more memorable than facts. Stories do the selling for us. We don't have to tell people what to do; we can tell them a story so they see what or what not to do on their own.

SELLING PAST THE CLOSE

Have you ever sold past the close? You told someone a story or got them to a tipping point or new beginning, and you still tried to sell to them. This is called selling past the close. When we do this, we go backward in the conversation.

Stories will do the selling for you if you let them. After I shared my story with Kelly and she then said that it was really helpful, I didn't go back and try to tell her why knowing your audience is the key to success.

Kelly already got the point and was ready to figure out what story she could share with her employee. Let the story do the work. It will save you a lot of time. Even if Kelly went back to her employee without her own story to tell her, she could tell my story to make the point of being aware of her surroundings. The story sticks and lives in the subconscious; it's memorable and repeatable, and will have the same effect.

STORYTELLING AND ATTENTION

How long do you have to tell a story and make your point in business? I get this question a lot. It's a little bit like videos on social media. Not that many years ago, you could post a three- or four-minute video and people had an appetite to watch it. The digital world is changing our attention span for how long we are willing to watch a video or listen to a story. The time is getting shorter and shorter.

My answer is it depends on context. If you are in a meeting, it might be one thing. If you are giving a presentation, it would be another and so on. More than anything, the listener will give you more time if you are telling a relevant and compelling story. You must take them on the path with you and guide them where you want them to go to keep their attention.

Following the path and guiding the listener to every milestone along the way ensures that the listener follows in your footsteps. When you know where you are on the path, they do too, which helps the listener relate and pay attention since they don't feel lost.

In business, you have anywhere from ten to thirty seconds to grab someone's attention and two to three minutes to tell a story that makes your point. If you are giving a presentation or a speech, your story could be five minutes to an hour.

STARTING WITH THE ENDING

One way to get someone to listen to your three-minute story is to start with the ending or the result. It's called the hook in marketing or sales terms.... For example, "We helped a customer reduce their sales cycle from six months to six weeks by transforming how they listen to their customers."

This is the ending, or new beginning of one of our stories at EQuipt. Once the listener says, "I'd like to hear more," the gate opens to go back to the beginning and share the entire story.

Another example is with email, whether a few sentences or a long paragraph. To be most effective, email should be constructed as stories using the stops corresponding to where you are on the path. The email subject line is the point of your email or story. When you start with the end in mind, you let the recipient, or the listener, know where you need them to go so they can prioritize and determine if a response is needed and how quickly.

STARTING WITH A FEW

What stories do you need in business? It can be overwhelming to think about all the stories you need to tell in various business conversations and situations. Since this is not a natural skill for most, the idea of having to build a large inventory of stories can feel daunting.

You really don't need one hundred stories; you just need to start with a few key ones. Build a few key stories first. Get good at telling them. You can use the same stories repeatedly if you are using them with different audiences.

About five years ago, we worked with the Germantown Academy grade school team. Sue had just hired a new assistant head of the grade school, Allison. She started just a few days prior to us conducting a Listening Path workshop. We had two sessions, training half the team the first week, the remainder the second week. Sue and Allison attended both sessions.

During the second session, we took a short break, and Allison said, "At first, I couldn't believe you were telling some of the same stories you told last week. But then I realized you don't need different stories for different audiences. Even though I heard them last week, I still got something new out of them."

You don't need to reinvent the wheel every time. When you have a story that makes a certain point and works, your brain will remember it when the situation arises. You just need to use the path and keep putting more stories in your backpack.

STORIES FOR YOUR BACKPACK

When you are on the trail, you will need stories in your backpack to help guide the other hikers to the new beginning. You'll need stories about you, your business, your customers, your employees, your failures, and the lessons you have learned. Be sure to think about the point you need to make for your listener as you build these stories.

The point of your story always has to focus on what's in it for the listener; otherwise, it's just a fun story. Then go back and gather from yourself what you need, one milestone or stop at a time, to make that point. Also, be sure to include both facts and feelings along the way. Let's look at some different types of stories you can use.

Vision/Strategy Story

A vision/strategy story is a story about a new beginning and painting a picture of the future. This could be the vision of the five-year plan for your company, the vision for a new process, the strategy for making more sales. It could be the vision of why Mom is taking a new job and moving the family to a different state.

The vision and strategy story helps others see where you are going together. Where did the story begin, what struggles have you gone through, and where do you need to go to create a better future? Paint a picture of the path you have traveled and the one you see ahead.

Company Story

This is a story about why your company exists and what you believe as a company. Where, when, why, and who founded the company? What struggles have you gone through? What challenges have you overcome to serve your customers? What do you deliver or do today? What's in it for customers if they choose you?

Purpose Story

This is a story about you and your purpose. Why do you do what you do? Where and when did your purpose begin? This is *not* about what you do, and it is *not* your resume. This is the story of what's in it for your listener and why they should believe in and buy from you.

Best Failure/Lessons Learned Story

This is a story about when you made a mistake or failed and either learned something or changed you in some way. (This can be in business or your personal life.) You are the main character; the story is about you. The more details (i.e., people, events, feelings, etc.), the better.

Customer Hero Story

This is a story about an experience you had when you helped a customer with a real business problem. Paint the picture of the beginning. Who was your customer hero, their title, their role? What were their struggles, including on the bottom line, who was affected, and how they felt? How did the customer partner with you to solve their problem?

The hero in this story is your *customer*, not you. The customer is the hero because they were the one who took the risk to change and used your product or services to make that change effective. What was the outcome or result? The more detail (i.e., people, events, feelings, etc.), the better.

Employee Hero Story

This is a story about an employee who did something that made a difference, internally or externally. Paint the picture of the beginning. Who was your employee hero, what was their title, their role? What were their struggles, including the cost? Who was affected, and how did they feel? How did the employee help with the problem or make a difference? What was the outcome? The more detail (i.e., people, events, feelings, etc.), the better.

Painting the Picture Story

This is a mini-story or a story within a conversation that paints a visual picture with words to make a point. For example, "It was like the customer was in a dark tunnel without a flashlight," or "It sounds like you felt punched in the gut." Use words to paint a visual picture to help the listener emotionally relate to the point.

PRACTICING YOUR WAY TO SUCCESS

Have you ever noticed that things can be harder than they look? I guarantee if someone is making something look easy, it's likely they have put in a lot of effort and work to do so. This is certainly true with storytelling.

About six years ago, one of my doctors asked me to do a video testimonial to tell the story of how he helped me. Bill Moss is an upper cervical chiropractor, one of only 200 in the country. This man was the missing link in getting my health back to a better place. He dramatically changed my life within three weeks of my first treatment. I was able to do things I hadn't been able to do in twenty years. I said, "Hell, yes, I'll do the testimonial."

I've been a storyteller my whole life, and I am in the business of story, so you might think it would be a breeze for me to summarize a twenty-year, complicated saga, down to three minutes. Wrong!

Telling a story that makes the right point is hard. I've learned the process is much simpler if I use the tools I've given you. I got out my story map, mapped out the path, gathered my own story, and put it on paper, making sure I made the right point. I brought my map on the day of the video shoot and practiced the story about eight times on the forty-minute drive to Bill's office.

When I sat down in front of the camera, the videographer said, "We can always edit so don't worry." Bill sat in front of me, and I told him my story rather than looking into the camera. After I told my story, the videographer said, "Wow, I can't believe we got that in one take." I responded, "Oh, that wasn't the first take. I probably spent about three hours developing the story and practiced eight times on the way here."

Bill and the videographer both laughed. While I appreciated that the videographer thought it took little effort to get the testimonial in one take, a lot of effort went into making it look effortless.

STORY AS A SECOND LANGUAGE

Did you know you are now well on your way to being proficient in the language of story? The path to gathering a story is the same path you need to build and tell stories. Story Gathering is the language of understanding, finding meaning, and joining the teller and the gatherer on the same path—creating a connection, a bond. Storytelling is the language of painting pictures with words to help others see another way and guide them to the solution or new beginning—helping someone overcome obstacles and fear of change.

People don't like to be told what to do. It creates resistance and can be tremendously costly. When you combine both Story Gathering and storytelling in your conversations, you begin not just to use story as a tool but to speak a language that is universally relatable.

Story is the language that transforms how we listen, talk, and understand ourselves and others, and it develops our emotional quotient and skills. Emotional skills make us great. Following the Listening Path to transform how you listen, understand, tell, influence, present yourself, and raise your EQ will ultimately transform how you connect, influence, solve, sell, and ultimately, succeed in life and at work.

EXERICISE

Write down your five biggest takeaways from this book.

_____

_____

_____

_____

_____

CHAPTER SUMMARY

1. Knowing how to effectively tell a story, like listening, is a skill that is underdeveloped and must be learned.

2. The Listening Path helps you to gather, build, and tell a story. Story Gathering and storytelling are inextricably linked. The path to success is the same for both.

3. Once you have earned the right to solve the problem, telling a story is the most effective way to do it. We call this story selling; the story will do the selling for you.

4. In our personal lives, our stories don't necessarily have to

make a point, but in business they do.

5. You need a variety of stories in your backpack to make the right point for your audiences. Build one story at a time, and take each one out when you need it. Eventually, you will have all the stories you need to make the right points.

6. You have ten seconds to three minutes to tell a story in a conversation. If you are giving a speech or presentation, your stories can be longer.

7. Story is a language. Learning to gather, tell, and weave story throughout your conversations is the universal language of influence.

"Listening is an art that requires attention over talent, spirit over ego, others over self."

— *Dean Jackson*

- A Final Note -

CREATING YOUR NEW BEGINNING

"The beginning is the most important part of the work."

— Plato

Now what? What new beginning do you want to create for your story?

Now that you have read my book, do you want to improve your relationship with your spouse, your kids, or your employees? Do you want to make more sales, drive more engagement in your organization, improve your EQ? Paint the picture of your new beginning in your mind. What area of your life would you like to change?

You now have the Listening Path system, including the tools. Not only the "what," but the "how" to transform your listening. You have at least half of the solution, but success will not come by accident. The other half will be creating the right habits. What habits are you ready to form to ensure your dreams come true? It will require taking the tools out of your backpack, using them, and walking the trail to success. Not to worry—you'll have tons of opportunities to practice listening differently. According to my research, people spend between 70 and 80 percent of their day engaged in some form of communication, and about 55 percent of their time is devoted to listening. You can practice with strangers, friends, family, employees—literally, anyone you meet.

My request is that before you continue any farther, you take out a pen or pencil, and in the lines provided below, write out the top ten actions to improve your listening that you plan to take in the next ninety days.

EXERCISE

Write ten actions you can commit to taking over the next ninety days. These actions are necessary to create the framework for living your life as you desire:

1. _____

2. _____

3. _____

4. _____

5. _____

6. _____

7. _____

8. _____

9. _____

10. _____

In this book, you have learned a new, game-changing paradigm for listening called *Story Gathering*, a transformational approach to listening that allows you to discover the hidden gems in conversations. You have learned to hear not only what is said but what is not said. By traveling this path, you will connect with the teller, find the meaning of the story, and earn the right to help them solve their problems.

You now understand how to identify your listening persona, know exactly when the unhelpful defense attorney shows up, and how to use the Listening Path tools to soothe your subconscious so you can listen differently without having to think about it. The meaning, the message, and the insight of the story will find you.

You have been shown the Listening Path framework and the five tools you need to transform how you listen. The path ensures that you do not get confused gathering a story and guides you and the teller to the new beginning to accomplish your goal. That goal can be to solve a disagreement, be more loving, make a sale...you name it. You have learned how to read the map that guides you on the path, how direct questions interfere with listening, and how you will have more success by using just six indirect questions, the ones that master story gatherers, journalists, and therapists use.

You have learned how to *reflect* what you heard in thirty to ninety seconds so you can sift all the story ingredients, much like when we are sifting the ingredients to bake a cake. You've learned to blend the right mix of facts, details, and emotions into your *reflection* to ensure understanding and meaning. You have learned how understanding and agreement have very little to do with one another. By affirming, you create alignment, break down walls and barriers, spark creativity, and help solve difficult problems. Finally, on the Listening Path, you have learned how to *mini-reflect* so you and the teller check in, following the same footsteps, and speeding up the process of getting to the story without getting lost.

When you follow the Listening Path, take out the tools from your backpack and practice using them, you will do more than transform how you listen. You will see the difference in how listening differently connects you to people, and the effect listening differently has on you and others.

You will transform how you present yourself to your family, friends, employees, and anyone you meet. You will recover the cost of *not* listening and by understanding you will connect, influence, and solve problems in the most powerful way. This will lead to greater success in both work and life.

Now that you have read my book, I encourage you to contact me to tell me what you liked and disliked so I can improve it for the next printing. More importantly, tell me about you, your challenges, your obstacles, and your adversity so I can help you. In fact, I would like to offer you a complimentary, no obligation, thirty- to sixty-minute consultation via phone, Zoom, Teams, or in person (if geography allows) to see how I can assist you in achieving your personal goals or organizational objectives.

My email address is Cmiles@EQuipt-People.com and my cell phone is 484-252-1593. Please email me, or better yet, text me with your name and time zone, and we will schedule your complimentary consultation. (I prefer texts to avoid spam blockers that prevent email communications.)

I wish you good luck! I hope your newly acquired listening skills will make your relationships at home and at work better. I also wish, as you give the gift of understanding, you will also receive it. Understanding is one of the greatest gifts you can give and/ or receive.

With a warm heart,

Christine

Christine

"The most important thing in communication is to hear what isn't being said."

— *Peter Drucker*

ABOUT THE AUTHOR

CHRISTINE MILES is an author, professional keynote speaker, consultant, executive coach, thought leader, entrepreneur, and radio show host. After a lifetime being intrigued with the concept of understanding others, she has become a recognized world expert in the field of listening differently.

For more than three decades, Christine has helped thousands of executives, individuals, and families expand human connections, transforming businesses and lives. She developed her gift of understanding others early in life as she watched her mother deal with adversity. She overcame learning challenges through her exceptional talent of listening differently and earned her BS in psychology at Millersville University and Master's in Psychology at the University of Pennsylvania. Christine received her certificate in Structural Family Therapy at the Philadelphia Child Guidance Center, part of the Hospital of the University of Pennsylvania.

Christine is a gifted, all-American field hockey athlete. She received the prestigious honor of being a Honda Broderick Award Nominee in 1987, a US field hockey squad member for two years, assistant coach at the University of Pennsylvania from 1989-1992, and inductee into the Millersville Hall of Fame in 2011.

Listening has helped Christine understand herself, her limitations, and her strengths, and driven her to a higher level of performance to persevere through life's obstacles. Listening differently prepared her for the hardest thing of all—reinventing herself at thirty-one after suffering a cervical spine injury in a car accident.

In 2019, Christine was the featured speaker at nine CIO and CFO forums across the US. She hosts the number-one business radio show on the East Coast, *Executive Leaders Radio*, where she has interviewed scores of CEOs about how their early life shaped their leadership. Christine is also the co-author of the book *The Art of the Nudge: Unlocking Your Hidden Potential*.

Christine founded her consulting and training business, EQuipt, to help leaders from medium-sized companies to Fortune 100 corporations grow sales, develop people, and create cultures of understanding. She also created her workshop *The Listening Path*, a transformational approach to understanding and insight.

Christine continues to dedicate her life to helping people and organizations achieve greater success through developing their emotional skills. She seeks to learn, loves hitting any ball (golf, tennis, ping pong, you name it), sharing her life with her boyfriend, Dean, and is the proud aunt of Elizabeth, Ashley, Lindsey, Kristen, and Maisey. Christine lives in a suburb of Philadelphia, Pennsylvania.

ABOUT CHRISTINE MILES COACHING

Why do world-class athletes have a professional coach? Do you want to maximize your potential and talent? Do you want to elevate your executive presence, improve how you lead, and get others to follow? Are you interested in learning how to get things done through people more effectively and how to leverage their talents to the fullest? Do you want to improve your personal brand? Do you know how to make your brand more powerful, tell your story, or craft a vision?

Christine Miles has been profoundly successful in coaching hundreds of people and dozens of executives over the course of her career. She has worked with leaders to help grow sales, uncover insights, deliver on business needs, develop people, and create transformative cultures. Christine uniquely takes a systemic approach so that not only you, but your organization is changed for the better. She can help you elevate your EQ; she can help you improve how you communicate your company strengths, talk about your products and your vision, and increase your customer successes. As a result of her coaching, you will learn how to listen differently, lead more effectively, close more sales, and achieve your personal and professional goals.

For more information, visit her website, www.EQuipt-People.com, and then text Christine your name and time zone to schedule your complimentary thirty- to sixty-minute, no-obligation consultation via phone, Zoom, Teams, or in-person (if geographically possible). You can email her, but she prefers you text her to ensure spam filters don't block your message.

www.EQuipt-People.com

Cmiles@EQuipt-People.com

484-252-1593

ABOUT EQUIPT TRAINING, CONSULTING, AND COACHING

What is it costing you and your organization *not* to listen?

Are you losing sales and customers? Are your employees disengaged? Is your IT team delivering what the business asks for instead of what it needs? Are your salespeople differentiating themselves, listening more than they talk, and uncovering the insights that drive high value sales? Do you want to elevate the emotional skills of your leaders, teams, employees, and salespeople?

EQuipt's mission is to deliver business and personal results by elevating your team's human skills. We believe empowering people with practical tools that elevate their understanding and emotional capabilities will transform them into more deliberate and dynamic team members and leaders. EQuipt was founded on the belief that *understanding* is key to success and so are our core values of driving results, trust, curiosity, empathy, and winning.

EQuipt has transformed thousands of employees and hundreds of teams ranging from medium-size companies to Fortune 100 corporations across all industries. EQuipt customizes our workshops, consultations, and coaching programs to solve your organization's specific problems and challenges, and improve *how* your people get things done.

EQuipt transforms *how* your employees and leaders listen to customers, prospects, key stakeholders, and each other. Transformational listening enables your team to uncover underlying problems, gain trust, earn credibility, and consistently provide smarter solutions. EQuipt's listening gurus coach your teams on how to apply these new tools and skills in their everyday lives, immediately improving your individual and organizational results.

For more information, visit our website, www.EQuipt-People. com, and then text Christine your name and time zone to schedule your complimentary, thirty- to sixty-minute, no-obligation consultation by phone, Zoom, Teams, or in-person (if geographically possible). You can email her, but she prefers you text her to ensure spam filters don't block your message.

www.EQuipt-People.com
Cmiles@EQuipt-People.com
484-252-1593

BOOK CHRISTINE MILES TO SPEAK AT YOUR NEXT EVENT

When it comes to choosing a professional speaker for your next event, you will find no one who will so renew your audience or colleagues' sense of passion and purpose than Christine Miles. Since 1991, Christine has delivered thousands of inspirational and actionable presentations worldwide. Whether your audience is ten or 10,000, in North America or abroad, Christine Miles can deliver a customized inspirational and informative message for your meeting or conference.

Christine understands your audience does not want to be *told* anything, but rather is interested in hearing stories and being part of the conversation. As a result, her speaking philosophy is to use humor, to entertain, and to engage audiences with passion and stories proven to help people and businesses achieve extraordinary results.

If you are looking for a memorable speaker who will leave your audience wanting more, book Christine Miles today! To find out whether Christine is available for your next meeting, visit her website, www.EQuipt-People.com.

Contact Christine by text to schedule a complimentary prespeech phone interview. You can email her; however, she prefers you text her to ensure spam filters don't block your message.

www.EQuipt-People.com

Cmiles@EQuipt-People.com

484-252-1593

"I remind myself every morning nothing I say this day will teach me more of anything. So, if I'm going to learn, I must do it by listening."

— *Larry King*